Hands-On Deep Learning with TensorFlow

Uncover what is underneath your data!

Dan Van Boxel

BIRMINGHAM - MUMBAI

Hands-On Deep Learning with TensorFlow

First published: July 2017

Production reference: 1280717

Published by Packt Publishing Ltd.
Livery Place
35 Livery Street
Birmingham B3 2PB, UK.
ISBN 978-1-78728-277-3

www.packtpub.com

Credits

Author
Dan Van Boxel

Commissioning Editor
Ben Renow-Clarke

Acquisition Editor
Ben Renow-Clarke

Content Development Editor
Radhika Atitkar

Technical Editor
Bhagyashree Rai

Copy Editor
Tom Jacob

Project Coordinator
Suzanne Coutinho

Proofreader
Safis Editing

Indexer
Tejal Daruwale Soni

Graphics
Kirk D'Penha

Production Coordinator
Arvindkumar Gupta

About the Author

Dan Van Boxel is a data scientist and machine learning engineer with over 10 years of experience. He is most well-known for `Dan Does Data`, a YouTube livestream demonstrating the power and pitfalls of neural networks. He has developed and applied novel statistical models of machine learning to topics such as accounting for truck traffic on highways, travel time outlier detection, and other areas. Dan has also published research articles and presented findings at the Transportation Research Board and other academic journals.

www.PacktPub.com

eBooks, discount offers, and more

Did you know that Packt offers eBook versions of every book published, with PDF and ePub files available? You can upgrade to the eBook version at www.PacktPub.com and as a print book customer, you are entitled to a discount on the eBook copy. Get in touch with us at customercare@packtpub.com for more details.

At www.PacktPub.com, you can also read a collection of free technical articles, sign up for a range of free newsletters and receive exclusive discounts and offers on Packt books and eBooks.

https://www.packtpub.com/mapt

Get the most in-demand software skills with Mapt. Mapt gives you full access to all Packt books and video courses, as well as industry-leading tools to help you plan your personal development and advance your career.

Why subscribe?

- Fully searchable across every book published by Packt
- Copy and paste, print, and bookmark content
- On demand and accessible via a web browser

Customer Feedback

Thanks for purchasing this Packt book. At Packt, quality is at the heart of our editorial process. To help us improve, please leave us an honest review on this book's Amazon page at `https://www.amazon.com/dp/1787282775`.

If you'd like to join our team of regular reviewers, you can email us at `customerreviews@packtpub.com`. We award our regular reviewers with free eBooks and videos in exchange for their valuable feedback. Help us be relentless in improving our products!

Table of Contents

Preface

TensorFlow is an open source software library for machine learning and training neural networks. TensorFlow was originally developed by Google, and was made open source in 2015.

Over the course of this book, you will learn how to use TensorFlow to solve a novel research problem. You'll use one of the most popular machine learning approaches, neural networks with TensorFlow. We'll work on both the simple and deep neural networks to improve our models.

You'll study images of letters and digits in various fonts with the goal of identifying fonts based on one specific image of a single letter. This will be a straightforward classification problem.

As no single pixel or position — but local structures among pixels — is important, it's an ideal problem for deep learning with TensorFlow. Though we'll start with simple models, this series will gradually introduce more nuanced approaches and explain the code line by line. By the end of this book, you'll have created your own advanced model for font recognition.

So let's put on our helmets; we're going deep into data mines with TensorFlow.

What this book covers

Chapter 1, Getting Started, discusses the techniques and the models we'll apply using TensorFlow. In this chapter, we will install TensorFlow on a machine we can use. After some small steps with basic computations, we will jump into a machine learning problem, successfully building a decent model with just logistic regression and a few lines of TensorFlow code.

Chapter 2, Deep Neural Networks, shows TensorFlow in its prime with deep neural networks. You will learn about the single and multiple hidden layer model. You will also learn about the different types of neural networks and build and train our first neural network with TensorFlow.

Chapter 3, Convolutional Neural Networks, talks about the most powerful developments in deep learning and applies the concepts of convolution to a simple example in TensorFlow. We will tackle the practical aspects of understanding convolution. We will explain what a convolutional and pooling layer is in a neural net, following with a TensorFlow example.

Chapter 4, Introducing Recurrent Neural Networks, introduces the concept of RNN models, and their implementation in TensorFlow. We will look at a simple interface to TensorFlow called TensorFlow learn. We will also walk through dense neural networks as well as understand convolutional neural networks and extracting weights in detail.

Chapter 5, Wrapping Up, wraps up our look at TensorFlow. We'll revisit our TensorFlow models for font classification, and review their accuracy.

What you need for this book

While this book will show you how to install TensorFlow, there are a few dependencies you need to be aware of. At a minimum, you need a recent version of Python 2 or 3 and NumPy. To get the most out of the book, you should also have Matplotlib and IPython.

Who this book is for

With deep learning going mainstream, making sense of data and getting accurate results using deep networks is possible. Dan Van Boxel is your guide to exploring the possibilities with deep learning; he will enable you to understand data like never before. With the efficiency and simplicity of TensorFlow, you will be able to process your data and gain insights that will change how you look at data.

Conventions

In this book, you will find a number of styles of text that distinguish between different kinds of information. Here are some examples of these styles, and an explanation of their meaning.

Code words in text, database table names, folder names, filenames, file extensions, pathnames, dummy URLs, user input, and Twitter handles are shown as follows: "The first thing you need to do is download the source code pack for this book and open the `simple.py` file."

A block of code is set as follows:

```
import tensorflow as tf
# You can create constants in TF to hold specific values
a = tf.constant(1)
b = tf.constant(2)
```

When we wish to draw your attention to a particular part of a code block, the relevant lines or items are set in bold:

```
import tensorflow as tf
# You can create constants in TF to hold specific values
a = tf.constant(1)
b = tf.constant(2)
```

Any command-line input or output is written as follows:

```
sudo pip3 install ./tensorflow-1.2.1-cp35-cp35m-linux_x86_64.
whl
```

New terms and **important words** are shown in bold. Words that you see on the screen, in menus or dialog boxes for example, appear in the text like this: "Click on **+New** to create a new file. Here we'll create a Jupyter notebook".

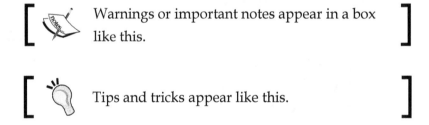

> Warnings or important notes appear in a box like this.

> Tips and tricks appear like this.

Reader feedback

Feedback from our readers is always welcome. Let us know what you think about this book—what you liked or may have disliked. Reader feedback is important for us to develop titles that you really get the most out of.

To send us general feedback, simply send an email to `feedback@packtpub.com`, and mention the book title via the subject of your message.

If there is a topic that you have expertise in and you are interested in either writing or contributing to a book, see our author guide on `www.packtpub.com/authors`.

Customer support

Now that you are the proud owner of a Packt book, we have a number of things to help you to get the most from your purchase.

Downloading the example code

You can download the example code files for this book from your account at `http://www.packtpub.com`. If you purchased this book elsewhere, you can visit `http://www.packtpub.com/support` and register to have the files e-mailed directly to you.

You can download the code files by following these steps:

1. Log in or register to our website using your e-mail address and password.
2. Hover the mouse pointer on the **SUPPORT** tab at the top.
3. Click on **Code Downloads & Errata**.

4. Enter the name of the book in the **Search** box.

5. Select the book for which you're looking to download the code files.

6. Choose from the drop-down menu where you purchased this book from.

7. Click on **Code Download**.

You can also download the code files by clicking on the **Code Files** button on the book's webpage at the Packt Publishing website. This page can be accessed by entering the book's name in the **Search** box. Please note that you need to be logged in to your Packt account.

Once the file is downloaded, please make sure that you unzip or extract the folder using the latest version of:

- WinRAR / 7-Zip for Windows
- Zipeg / iZip / UnRarX for Mac
- 7-Zip / PeaZip for Linux

The code bundle for the book is also hosted on GitHub at `https://github.com/PacktPublishing/Hands-On-Deep-Learning-with-TensorFlow`. We also have other code bundles from our rich catalog of books and videos available at `https://github.com/PacktPublishing/`. Check them out!

Downloading the color images of this book

We also provide you with a PDF file that has color images of the screenshots/diagrams used in this book. The color images will help you better understand the changes in the output. You can download this file from `https://www.packtpub.com/sites/default/files/HandsOnDeepLearningwithTensorFlow.pdf`.

Errata

Although we have taken every care to ensure the accuracy of our content, mistakes do happen. If you find a mistake in one of our books — maybe a mistake in the text or the code — we would be grateful if you could report this to us. By doing so, you can save other readers from frustration and help us improve subsequent versions of this book. If you find any errata, please report them by visiting `http://www.packtpub.com/submit-errata`, selecting your book, clicking on the **Errata Submission Form** link, and entering the details of your errata. Once your errata are verified, your submission will be accepted and the errata will be uploaded to our website or added to any list of existing errata under the Errata section of that title.

To view the previously submitted errata, go to `https://www.packtpub.com/books/content/support` and enter the name of the book in the search field. The required information will appear under the **Errata** section.

Piracy

Piracy of copyrighted material on the Internet is an ongoing problem across all media. At Packt, we take the protection of our copyright and licenses very seriously. If you come across any illegal copies of our works in any form on the Internet, please provide us with the location address or website name immediately so that we can pursue a remedy.

Please contact us at copyright@packtpub.com with a link to the suspected pirated material.

We appreciate your help in protecting our authors and our ability to bring you valuable content.

Questions

If you have a problem with any aspect of this book, you can contact us at questions@packtpub.com, and we will do our best to address the problem.

1
Getting Started

TensorFlow is a new machine learning and graph computation library recently released by Google. Its Python interface ensures the elegant design of common models, while its compiled backend ensures speed.

Let's take a glimpse at the techniques you'll learn and the models you'll build as you apply TensorFlow.

Installing TensorFlow

In this section, you will learn what TensorFlow is, how to install it, and how to build simple models and do simple computations. Further, you will learn how to build a logistic regression model for classification, and introduce a machine learning problem to help us learn TensorFlow.

We're going to learn what kind of library TensorFlow is and install it on our own Linux machine, or a free instance of CoCalc if you don't have access to a Linux machine.

TensorFlow – main page

First, what is TensorFlow? TensorFlow is a new machine learning library put out by Google. It is designed to be very easy to use and is very fast. If you go to the TensorFlow website, `tensorflow.org`, you will have access to a wealth of information about what TensorFlow is and how to use it. We'll be referring to this often, particularly the documentation.

TensorFlow – the installation page

Before we get started with TensorFlow, note that you need to install it, as it probably doesn't come preinstalled on your operating system. So, if you go to the **Install** tab on the TensorFlow web page, click on **Installing TensorFlow on Ubuntu**, and then click on **"native" pip**, you will learn how to install TensorFlow.

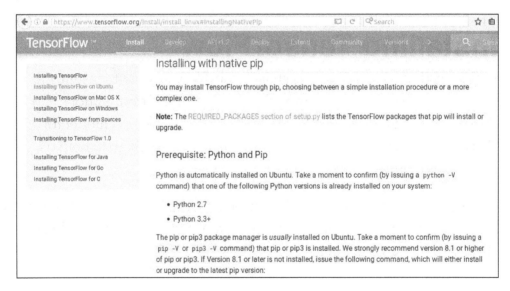

Installing TensorFlow is very challenging, even for experienced system administrators. So, I highly recommend using something like the `pip` installation; alternatively, if you're familiar with Docker, use the Docker installation. You can install TensorFlow from the source, but this can be very difficult. We will install TensorFlow using a precompiled binary called a **wheel file**. You can install this file using Python's `pip` module installer.

Installing via pip

For the `pip` installation, you have the option of using either a Python 2 or Python 3 version. Also, you can choose between the CPU and GPU version. If your computer has a powerful graphics card, the GPU version may be for you.

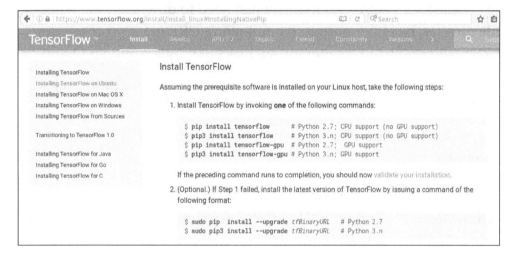

However, you need to check that your graphics card is compatible with TensorFlow. If it's not, it's fine; everything in this series can be done with just the CPU version.

We can install TensorFlow by using the `pip install tensorflow` command (based on your CPU or GPU support and `pip` version), as shown in the preceding screenshot.

So, if you copy the following line for TensorFlow, you can install it as well:

```
# Python 3.4 installation
sudo pip3 install --upgrade \
https://storage.googleapis.com/tensorflow/linux/cpu/
tensorflow-1.2.1-cp34-cp34m-linux_x86_64.whl
```

If you don't have Python 3.4, as the wheel file called for, that's okay. You can probably still use the same wheel file. Let's take a look at how to do this for Python 3.5. First, you just need to download the wheel file directly, by either putting the following URL in your browser or using a command-line program, such as wget, as we're doing here:

```
wget  https://storage.googleapis.com/tensorflow/linux/cpu/
tensorflow-1.2.1-cp34-cp34m-linux_x86_64.whl
```

If you download this, it will very quickly be grabbed by your computer.

Now all you need to do is change the name of the file from cp34, which stands for Python 3.4, to whichever version of Python 3 you're using. In this case, we'll change it to a version using Python 3.5, so we'll change 4 to 5:

```
mv tensorflow-1.2.1-cp34-cp34m-linux_x86_64.whl tensorflow-
1.2.1-cp35-cp35m-linux_x86_64.whl
```

Now you can install TensorFlow for Python 3.5 by simply changing the installation line here to `pip3 install` and the name of the new wheel file after changing it to 3.5:

```
sudo pip3 install ./tensorflow-1.2.1-cp35-cp35m-linux_x86_64.
whl
```

We can see this works just fine. Now you've installed TensorFlow.

```
😊😊😊  bhagya@bhagya-VirtualBox: ~/Downloads
bhagya@bhagya-VirtualBox:~/Downloads$ sudo pip3 install ./tensorflow-1.2.1-cp35-
cp35m-linux_x86_64.whl
The directory '/home/bhagya/.cache/pip/http' or its parent directory is not owne
d by the current user and the cache has been disabled. Please check the permissi
ons and owner of that directory. If executing pip with sudo, you may want sudo's
 -H flag.
The directory '/home/bhagya/.cache/pip' or its parent directory is not owned by
the current user and caching wheels has been disabled. check the permissions and
 owner of that directory. If executing pip with sudo, you may want sudo's -H fla
g.
Processing ./tensorflow-1.2.1-cp35-cp35m-linux_x86_64.whl
Collecting html5lib==0.9999999 (from tensorflow==1.2.1)
  Downloading html5lib-0.9999999.tar.gz (889kB)
    100% |                              | 890kB 129kB/s
Collecting bleach==1.5.0 (from tensorflow==1.2.1)
  Downloading bleach-1.5.0-py2.py3-none-any.whl
Requirement already satisfied (use --upgrade to upgrade): wheel>=0.26 in /usr/li
b/python3/dist-packages (from tensorflow==1.2.1)
Requirement already satisfied (use --upgrade to upgrade): six>=1.10.0 in /usr/li
b/python3/dist-packages (from tensorflow==1.2.1)
Collecting numpy>=1.11.0 (from tensorflow==1.2.1)
  Downloading numpy-1.13.1-cp35-cp35m-manylinux1_x86_64.whl (16.9MB)
    100% |                              | 16.9MB 51kB/s
Collecting protobuf>=3.2.0 (from tensorflow==1.2.1)
```

If your installation somehow becomes corrupted later, you can always jump back to this segment to remind yourself about the steps involved in the installation.

Installing via CoCalc

If you don't have administrative or installation rights on your computer but still want to try TensorFlow, you can try running TensorFlow over the web in a CoCalc instance. If you go to `https://cocalc.com/` and create a new account, you can create a new project. This will give you a sort of a virtual machine that you can play around with. Conveniently, TensorFlow is already installed in the Anaconda 3 kernel.

Let's create a new project called `TensorFlow`. Click on **+Create new project…**, enter a title for your project, and click on **Create Project**. Now we can go into our project by clicking on the title. It will take a couple of seconds to load.

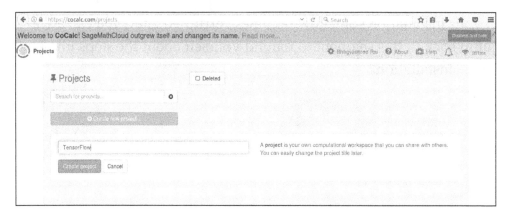

Click on **+New** to create a new file. Here, we'll create a Jupyter notebook:

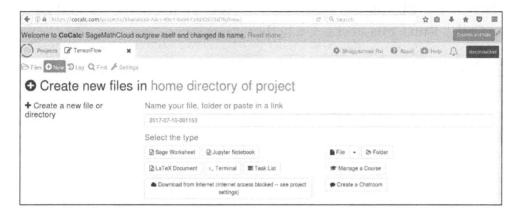

Jupyter is a convenient way to interact with IPython and the primary means of using CoCalc for these computations. It may take a few seconds to load.

When you get to the interface shown in the following screenshot, the first thing you need to do is change the kernel to Anaconda Python 3 by going to **Kernel | Change kernel... | Python 3 (Anaconda)**:

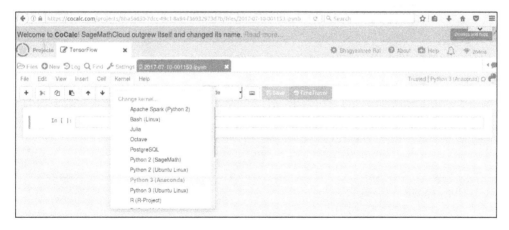

This will give you the proper dependencies to use TensorFlow. It may take a few seconds for the kernel to change. Once you are connected to the new kernel, you can type `import tensorflow` in the cell and go to **Cell** | **Run Cells** to check whether it works:

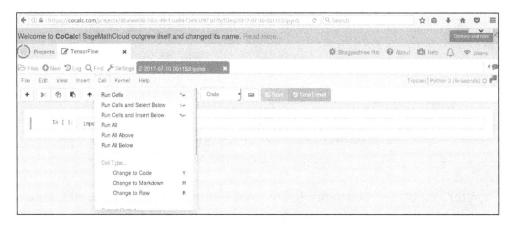

If your Jupyter notebook takes a long time to load, you can instead create a Terminal in CoCalc using the button shown in the following screenshot:

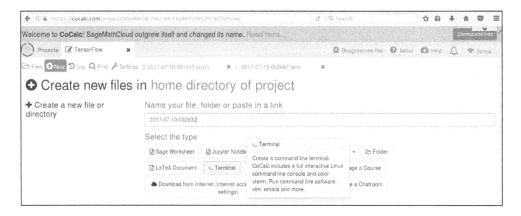

Once there, type `anaconda3` to switch environments, then type `ipython3` to launch an interactive Python session, as shown in the following screenshot:

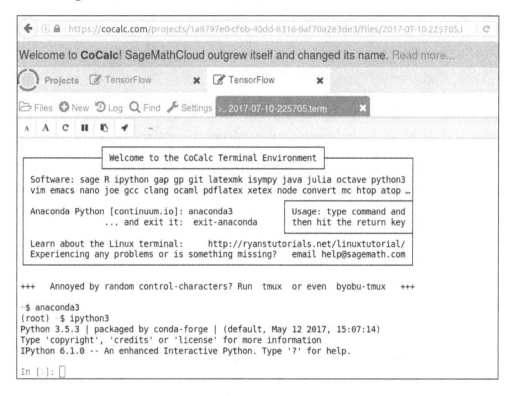

You can easily work here, although you won't be able to visualize the output. Type `import tensorflow` in the Terminal and off you go.

So far in this section, you've learned what TensorFlow is and how to install it, either locally or on a virtual machine on the web. Now we're ready to explore simple computations in TensorFlow.

Simple computations

First, we're going to take a look at the tensor object type. Then we'll have a graphical understanding of TensorFlow to define computations. Finally, we'll run the graphs with sessions, showing how to substitute intermediate values.

Defining scalars and tensors

The first thing you need to do is download the source code pack for this book and open the `simple.py` file. You can either use this file to copy and paste lines into TensorFlow or CoCalc, or type them directly yourselves. First, let's import `tensorflow` as `tf`. This is a convenient way to refer to it in Python. You'll want to hold your constant numbers in `tf.constant` calls. For example, let's do `a = tf.constant(1)` and `b = tf.constant(2)`:

```
import tensorflow as tf
# You can create constants in TF to hold specific values
a = tf.constant(1)
b = tf.constant(2)
```

Of course, you can add and multiply these to get other values, namely c and d:

```
# Of course you can add, multiply, and compute on these as
you like
c = a + b
d = a * b
```

TensorFlow numbers are stored in **tensors**, a fancy term for multidimensional arrays. If you pass a Python list to TensorFlow, it does the right thing and converts it into an appropriately dimensioned tensor. You can see this illustrated in the following code:

```
# TF numbers are stored in "tensors", a fancy term for
multidimensional arrays. If you pass TF a Python list, it
can convert it
V1 = tf.constant([1., 2.])    # Vector, 1-dimensional
V2 = tf.constant([3., 4.])    # Vector, 1-dimensional
M = tf.constant([[1., 2.]])            # Matrix, 2d
N = tf.constant([[1., 2.],[3.,4.]])    # Matrix, 2d
K = tf.constant([[[1., 2.],[3.,4.]]])  # Tensor, 3d+
```

The V1 vector, a one-dimensional tensor, is passed as a Python list of [1. , 2.]. The dots here just force Python to store the number as decimal values rather than integers. The V2 vector is another Python list of [3. , 4.]. The M variable is a two-dimensional matrix made from a list of lists in Python, creating a two-dimensional tensor in TensorFlow. The N variable is also a two-dimensional matrix. Note that this one actually has multiple rows in it. Finally, K is a true tensor, containing three dimensions. Note that the final dimension contains just one entry, a single two-by-two box.

Don't worry if this terminology is a bit confusing. Whenever you see a strange new variable, you can jump back to this point to understand what it might be.

Computations on tensors

You can also do simple things, such as add tensors together:

```
V3 = V1 + V2
```

Alternatively, you can multiply them element-wise, so each common position is multiplied together:

```
# Operations are element-wise by default
M2 = M * M
```

For true matrix multiplication, however, you need to use `tf.matmul`, passing in your two tensors as arguments:

```
NN = tf.matmul(N,N)
```

Doing computation

Everything so far has just specified the TensorFlow graph; we haven't yet computed anything. To do this, we need to start a session in which the computations will take place. The following code creates a new session:

```
sess = tf.Session()
```

Once you have a session open, doing: `sess.run(NN)` will evaluate the given expression and return an array. We can easily send this to a variable by doing the following:

```
output = sess.run(NN)
print("NN is:")
print(output)
```

If you run this cell now, you should see the correct tensor array for the NN output on the screen:

When you're done using your session, it's good to close it, just like you would close a file handle:

```
# Remember to close your session when you're done using it
sess.close()
```

For interactive work, we can use `tf.InteractiveSession()` like so:

```
sess = tf.InteractiveSession()
```

You can then easily compute the value of any node. For example, entering the following code and running the cell will output the value of M2:

```
# Now we can compute any node
print("M2 is:")
print(M2.eval())
```

Variable tensors

Of course, not all our numbers are constant. To update weights in a neural network, for example, we need to use `tf.Variable` to create the appropriate object:

```
W = tf.Variable(0, name="weight")
```

Note that variables in TensorFlow are not initialized automatically. To do so, we need to use a special call, namely `tf.global_variables_initializer()`, and then run that call with `sess.run()`:

```
init_op = tf.global_variables_initializer()
sess.run(init_op)
```

This is to put a value in that variable. In this case, it will stuff a 0 value into the W variable. Let's just verify that W has that value:

```
print("W is:")
print(W.eval())
```

You should see an output value for W of 0 in your cell:

```
In [26]: print("W is:")
W is:

In [27]: print(W.eval())
0
```

Let's see what happens when you add a to it:

```
W += a
print("W after adding a:")
print(W.eval())
```

Recall that a is 1, so you get the expected value of 1 here:

```
In [28]: W += a

In [29]: print("W after adding a:")
W after adding a:

In [30]: print(W.eval())
1
```

Let's add a again, just to make sure we can increment and that it's truly a variable:

```
W += a
print("W after adding a:")
print(W.eval())
```

Now you should see that W is holding 2, as we have incremented it twice with a:

```
In [31]: W += a

In [32]: print("W after adding a again:")
W after adding a again:

In [33]: print(W.eval())
2

In [34]:
```

Viewing and substituting intermediate values

You can return or supply arbitrary nodes when doing a TensorFlow computation. Let's define a new node but also return another node at the same time in a fetch call. First, let's define our new node E, as shown here:

```
E = d + b # 1*2 + 2 = 4
```

Let's take a look at what E starts as:

```
print("E as defined:")
print(E.eval())
```

You should see that, as expected, E equals 4. Now let's see how we can pass in multiple nodes, E and d, to return multiple values from a sess.run call:

```
# Let's see what d was at the same time
print("E and d:")
print(sess.run([E,d]))
```

You should see multiple values, namely 4 and 2, returned in your output:

```
In [37]: print("E and d:")
E and d:

In [38]: print(sess.run([E,d]))
[4, 2]
```

Now suppose we want to use a different intermediate value, say for debugging purposes. We can use `feed_dict` to supply a custom value to a node anywhere in our computation when returning a value. Let's do that now with d equals 4 instead of 2:

```
# Use a custom d by specifying a dictionary
print("E with custom d=4:")
print(sess.run(E, feed_dict = {d:4.}))
```

Remember that E equals d + b and the values of d and b are both 2. Although we've inserted a new value of 4 for d, you should see that the value of E will now be output as 6:

```
In [39]: print("E with custom d=4:")
E with custom d=4:

In [40]: print(sess.run(E, feed_dict = {d:4.}))
6

In [41]:
```

You have now learned how to do core computations with TensorFlow tensors. It's time to take the next step forward by building a logistic regression model.

Logistic regression model building

Okay, let's get started with building a real machine learning model. First, we'll see the proposed machine learning problem: font classification. Then, we'll review a simple algorithm for classification, called **logistic regression**. Finally, we'll implement logistic regression in TensorFlow.

Introducing the font classification dataset

Before we jump in, let's load all the necessary modules:

```
import tensorflow as tf
import numpy as np
```

If you're copying and pasting to IPython, make sure your autoindent property is set to OFF:

```
%autoindent
```

The tqdm module is optional; it just shows nice progress bars:

```
try:
    from tqdm import tqdm
except ImportError:
    def tqdm(x, *args, **kwargs):
        return x
```

Next, we'll set a seed of 0, just to get consistent data splitting from run to run:

```
# Set random seed
np.random.seed(0)
```

In this book, we've provided a dataset of the images of characters using five fonts. For convenience, these are stored in a compressed NumPy file (data_with_labels.npz), which can be found in the download package of this book. You can easily load these into Python with numpy.load:

```
# Load data
data = np.load('data_with_labels.npz')
train = data['arr_0']/255.
labels = data['arr_1']
```

The `train` variable here holds the actual pixel values scaled from 0 to 1, and `labels` holds the type of font that it was; therefore, it'll be either 0, 1, 2, 3, or 4, as there are five fonts in total. You can print out these values, so you can look at them using the following code:

```
# Look at some data
print(train[0])
print(labels[0])
```

However, that's not very instructive, as most of the values are zeroes and only the central part of the screen contains the image data:

```
In [8]: print(train[0])
[[ 0.  0.  0. ...,  0.  0.  0.]
 [ 0.  0.  0. ...,  0.  0.  0.]
 [ 0.  0.  0. ...,  0.  0.  0.]
 ...,
 [ 0.  0.  0. ...,  0.  0.  0.]
 [ 0.  0.  0. ...,  0.  0.  0.]
 [ 0.  0.  0. ...,  0.  0.  0.]]

In [9]: print(labels[0])
0

In [10]:
```

If you have Matplotlib installed, now is a good place to import it. We'll use `plt.ion()` to automatically bring up figures when needed:

```
# If you have matplotlib installed
import matplotlib.pyplot as plt
plt.ion()
```

Here are some example images of characters from each font:

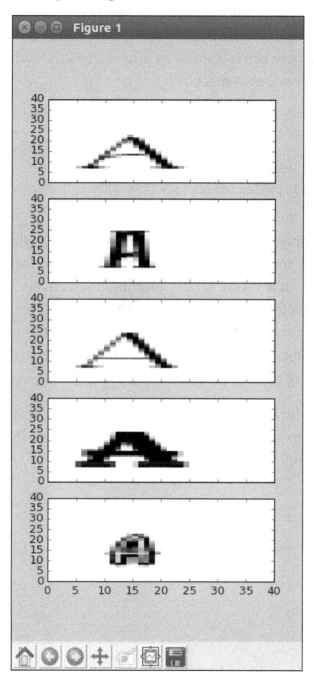

Yeah, they're pretty flashy. In the dataset, each image is represented as a 36 x 36 two-dimensional matrix of pixel darkness values. The 0 value represents a white pixel, while 255 represents a black pixel. Everything in between is a shade of gray. Here's the code to display these fonts on your own machine:

```
# Let's look at a subplot of one of A in each font
f, plts = plt.subplots(5, sharex=True)
c = 91
for i in range(5):
    plts[i].pcolor(train[c + i * 558],
                   cmap=plt.cm.gray_r)
```

If your plot appears really wide, you can easily resize the window just using your mouse. It's often much more work to resize it ahead of time in Python if you're simply plotting interactively. Our goal is to decide which font an image belongs to, given that we have many other labeled images of the fonts. To expand the dataset and help avoid overfitting, we have also *jittered* each character around in the 36 x 36 area, giving us nine times as many data points.

It may be helpful to come back to this after working with later models. It's important to keep the original data in mind, no matter how advanced the final model is.

Logistic regression

If you're familiar with linear regression, you're halfway toward understanding logistic regression. Basically, we're going to assign a weight to each pixel in the image, then take the weighted sum of those pixels (beta for weights and X for pixels). This will give us a score for that image being a particular font. Every font will have its own set of weights, as they will value pixels differently. To convert these scores into proper probabilities (represented by Y), we will use what's called the `softmax` function to force their sum to be between 0 and 1, as illustrated next. Whatever probability is the greatest for a particular image, we will classify it into the associated class.

You can read more about the theory of logistic regression in most statistical modeling textbooks. Here is its formula:

$$Pr(Y_i = c) = \frac{\beta_c X_i}{\sum_h \beta_h X_i}$$

One good reference that focuses on applications is William H. Greene's *Econometric Analysis, Pearson,* published in the year 2012.

Getting data ready

Implementing logistic regression is pretty easy in TensorFlow and will serve as scaffolding for more complex machine learning algorithms. First, we need to convert our integer labels into a *one-hot* format. This means, instead of labeling an image with font class 2, we transform the label into [0, 0, 1, 0, 0]. That is, we stick 1 in position two (note 0-up counting is common in computer science) and 0 for every other class. Here's the code for our `to_onehot` function:

```
def to_onehot(labels,nclasses = 5):
    '''
    Convert labels to "one-hot" format.
    >>> a = [0,1,2,3]
    >>> to_onehot(a,5)
    array([[ 1.,   0.,   0.,   0.,   0.],
           [ 0.,   1.,   0.,   0.,   0.],
           [ 0.,   0.,   1.,   0.,   0.],
           [ 0.,   0.,   0.,   1.,   0.]])
    '''
    outlabels = np.zeros((len(labels),nclasses))
    for i,l in enumerate(labels):
        outlabels[i,l] = 1
    return outlabels
```

With this done, we can go ahead and call the function:

```
onehot = to_onehot(labels)
```

For the pixels, we don't really want a matrix in this case, so we'll flatten the 36 x 36 numbers into a one-dimensional vector of length 1,296, but this will come a little bit later. Also, recall that we've rescaled the pixel values of 0-255 so that they fall between 0 and 1.

Okay, our final piece of preparation is to split our dataset into training and validation sets. This will help us catch overfitting later on. The training set will help us determine the weights in our logistic regression model, and the validation set will just be used to confirm that those weights are reasonably correct on new data:

```
# Split data into training and validation
indices = np.random.permutation(train.shape[0])
valid_cnt = int(train.shape[0] * 0.1)
test_idx, training_idx = indices[:valid_cnt],\
                         indices[valid_cnt:]
test, train = train[test_idx,:],\
              train[training_idx,:]
onehot_test, onehot_train = onehot[test_idx,:],\
                            onehot[training_idx,:]
```

Building a TensorFlow model

Okay, let's kick off the TensorFlow code by creating an interactive session:

```
sess = tf.InteractiveSession()
```

With this, we've started our first model in TensorFlow.

We're going to use a placeholder variable for x, which represents our input images. This is just to tell TensorFlow that we will supply the value for this node via feed_dict later on:

```
# These will be inputs
## Input pixels, flattened
x = tf.placeholder("float", [None, 1296])
```

Also, note that we can specify the shape of this tensor, and here we have used None as one of the sizes. The None size allows us to send an arbitrary number of data points into the algorithm at once for batch processing. We'll use the variable y_ likewise to hold our known labels to be used for training later on:

```
## Known labels
y_ = tf.placeholder("float", [None,5])
```

To perform logistic regression, we need a set of weights (W). In fact, we need 1,296 weights for each of the five font classes, which will give us our shape. Note that we also want to include an extra weight for each class as a bias (b). This is the same as adding an extra input variable that always takes the value 1:

```
# Variables
W = tf.Variable(tf.zeros([1296,5]))
b = tf.Variable(tf.zeros([5]))
```

With all these TensorFlow variables floating around, we need to make sure they get initialized. Let's call them now:

```
# Just initialize
sess.run(tf.global_variables_initializer())
```

Good job! You've got everything prepared. Now you can implement the softmax formula to compute probabilities. Because we set up our weights and input very carefully, TensorFlow makes this task very easy with just a call to tf.matmul and tf.nn.softmax:

```
# Define model
y = tf.nn.softmax(tf.matmul(x,W) + b)
```

That's it! You've implemented an entire machine learning classifier in TensorFlow. Nice work. But where do we get the values for the weights? Let's take a look at using TensorFlow to train the model.

Logistic regression training

First, you'll learn about the loss function for our machine learning classifier and implement it in TensorFlow. Then, we'll quickly train the model by evaluating the right TensorFlow node. Finally, we'll verify that our model is reasonably accurate and the weights make sense.

Developing the loss function

Optimizing our model really means minimizing how wrong we are. With our labels in *one-hot* style, it's easy to compare these with the class probabilities predicted by the model. The categorical `cross_entropy` function is a formal way to measure this. While the exact statistics are beyond the scope of this course, you can think of it as punishing the model for more for less accurate predictions. To compute it, we multiply our *one-hot* real labels element-wise with the natural log of the predicted probabilities, then sum these values and negate them. Conveniently, TensorFlow already includes this function as `tf.nn.softmax_cross_entropy_with_logits()` and we can just call that:

```
# Climb on cross-entropy
cross_entropy = tf.reduce_mean(
        tf.nn.softmax_cross_entropy_with_logits(
        logits = y + 1e-50, labels = y_))
```

Note that we are adding a small error value of `1e-50` here to avoid numerical instability problems.

Training the model

TensorFlow is convenient in that it provides built-in optimizers to take advantage of the loss function we just wrote. Gradient descent is a common choice and will slowly nudge our weights toward better results. This is the node that will update our weights:

```
# How we train
train_step = tf.train.GradientDescentOptimizer(
              0.02).minimize(cross_entropy)
```

Before we actually start training, we should specify a few more nodes to assess how well the model does:

```
# Define accuracy
correct_prediction = tf.equal(tf.argmax(y,1),
                      tf.argmax(y_,1))
accuracy = tf.reduce_mean(tf.cast(
          correct_prediction, "float"))
```

The `correct_prediction` node is 1 if our model assigns the highest probability to the correct class, and 0 otherwise. The `accuracy` variable averages these predictions over the available data, giving us an overall sense of how well the model did.

When training in machine learning, we often want to use the same data point multiple times to squeeze all the information out. Each pass through the entire training data is called an **epoch**. Here, we're going to save both the training and validation accuracy every 10 epochs:

```
# Actually train
epochs = 1000
train_acc = np.zeros(epochs//10)
test_acc = np.zeros(epochs//10)
for i in tqdm(range(epochs)):
    # Record summary data, and the accuracy
    if i % 10 == 0:
        # Check accuracy on train set
        A = accuracy.eval(feed_dict={
            x: train.reshape([-1,1296]),
            y_: onehot_train})
        train_acc[i//10] = A
        # And now the validation set
        A = accuracy.eval(feed_dict={
            x: test.reshape([-1,1296]),
            y_: onehot_test})
        test_acc[i//10] = A
    train_step.run(feed_dict={
        x: train.reshape([-1,1296]),
        y_: onehot_train})
```

Note that we use `feed_dict` to pass in different types of data to get different output values. Finally, `train_step.run` updates the model every iteration. This should only take a few minutes on a typical computer, much less if you're using a GPU, and a bit more on an underpowered machine.

You just trained a model with TensorFlow; awesome!

Evaluating the model accuracy

After 1,000 epochs, let's take a look at the model. If you have Matplotlib installed, you can view the accuracies in a graphical plot; if not, you can still look at the number. For the final results, use the following code:

```
# Notice that accuracy flattens out
print(train_acc[-1])
print(test_acc[-1])
```

If you do have Matplotlib installed, you can use the following code to display the plot:

```
# Plot the accuracy curves
plt.figure(figsize=(6,6))
plt.plot(train_acc, 'bo')
plt.plot(test_acc, 'rx')
```

You should see something like the following plot (note that we used some random initialization, so it might not be exactly the same):

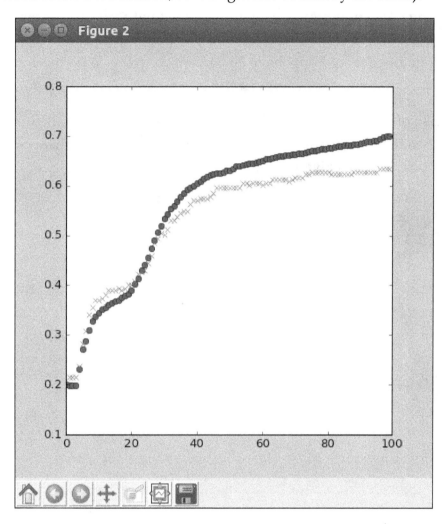

It seems like the validation accuracy flattens out after about 400-500 iterations; beyond this, our model may either be overfitting or not learning much more. Also, even though the final accuracy of about 40 percent might seem poor, recall that, with five classes, a totally random guess would only have 20 percent accuracy. With this limited dataset, the simple model is doing all it can.

It's also often helpful to look at computed weights. These can give you a clue as to what the model thinks is important. Let's plot them by pixel position for a given class:

```
# Look at a subplot of the weights for each font
f, plts = plt.subplots(5, sharex=True)
for i in range(5):
    plts[i].pcolor(W.eval()[:,i].reshape([36,36]))
```

This should give you a result similar to the following (again, if the plot comes out very wide, you can squeeze in the window size to square it up):

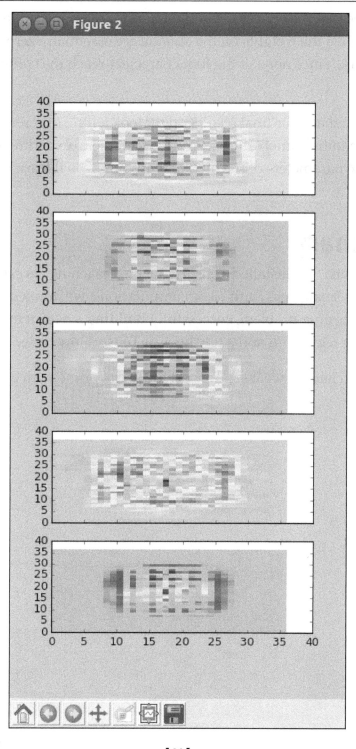

We can see that the weights near the interior are important in some models, while the weights on the outside are essentially zero. This makes sense, since none of the font characters reach the corners of the images.

Again, note that your final results might look a little different due to random initialization effects. Always feel free to experiment and change the parameters of the model; that's how you'll learn new things.

Summary

In this chapter, we installed TensorFlow on a machine we can use. After some small steps with basic computations, we jumped into a machine learning problem, successfully building a decent model with just logistic regression and a few lines of TensorFlow code.

In the next chapter, we'll see TensorFlow in its prime with deep neural networks.

2
Deep Neural Networks

In the previous chapter, we looked at simple TensorFlow operations and how to use logistic regression on our font classification problem. In this chapter, we will dive into one of the most popular and successful machine learning approaches—neural networks. Using TensorFlow, we'll build both simple and deep neural networks to improve our model of the font classification problem. Here, we will put the basics of neural networks into practice. We will also build and train our first neural network with TensorFlow. We will then move on to a neural network with a hidden layer of neurons and understand it completely. When completed, you will have a better grasp of the following topics:

- Basic neural networks
- The single hidden layer model
- The single hidden layer explained
- The multiple hidden layer model
- Results of the multiple hidden layer

In our first section, we'll review the basics of neural networks. You will learn common ways to transform input data, understand how neural networks connect these transformations, and finally, how to implement a single neuron in TensorFlow.

Basic neural networks

Our logistic regression model worked well enough, but was fundamentally linear in nature. Doubling the intensity of a pixel doubled its contribution to the score, but we might only really care if a pixel was above a certain threshold or put more weight on changes to small values. Linearity may not capture all the nuances of the problem. One way to handle this issue is to transform our input with a nonlinear function. Let's look at a simple example in TensorFlow.

First, be sure to load the required modules (`tensorflow`, `numpy`, and `math`) and start an interactive session:

```
import tensorflow as tf
import numpy as np
import math

sess = tf.InteractiveSession()
```

In the following example, we create three five-long vectors of normal random numbers, truncated to keep them from being too extreme, with different centers:

```
x1 = tf.Variable(tf.truncated_normal([5],
                mean=3, stddev=1./math.sqrt(5)))
x2 = tf.Variable(tf.truncated_normal([5],
                mean=-1, stddev=1./math.sqrt(5)))
x3 = tf.Variable(tf.truncated_normal([5],
                mean=0, stddev=1./math.sqrt(5)))

sess.run(tf.global_variables_initializer())
```

 Note that, because this is random, your values are probably going to be a little different, but that's perfectly fine.

A common transformation is to square the input. Doing this makes larger values even more extreme, and of course makes everything positive:

```
sqx2 = x2 * x2
print(x2.eval())
print(sqx2.eval())
```

You can see the result in the following screenshot:

```
In [11]: print(x2.eval())
[-1.59633303 -1.39370716 -1.11756158 -0.93147004 -1.30868506]

In [12]: print(sqx2.eval())
[ 2.54827905  1.94241965  1.24894392  0.86763644  1.71265662]

In [13]:
```

Log function

Conversely, if you need more nuance among your small values, you can try taking the natural or any base logarithm of your inputs:

```
logx1 = tf.log(x1)
print(x1.eval())
print(logx1.eval())
```

Refer to the following screenshot and note that large values tend to become squished together, while the smaller values are a little more spread out:

```
In [14]: print(x1.eval())
[ 3.2928977   3.11865115  2.75602937  2.55065155  2.60228252]

In [15]: print(logx1.eval())
[ 1.19176793  1.13740063  1.01379097  0.9363488   0.95638895]

In [16]:
```

However, logarithms can't handle negative inputs, and the closer you get to zero, the more extremely negative your small input becomes. Therefore, be careful with logarithms. Finally, there's the sigmoid transformation.

Sigmoid function

Don't worry about the formula, just know that extreme values, positive and negative, get squished to plus one or zero, respectively, and inputs closer to zero become closer to one-half:

```
sigx3 = tf.sigmoid(x3)
print(x3.eval())
print(sigx3.eval())
```

Here, you see an example that's become close to one-half. It started at one-quarter and is almost one-half now:

```
In [17]: print(x3.eval())
[-0.24215472 -0.26575294 -0.30768225  0.0072251  -0.1542311 ]

In [18]: print(sigx3.eval())
[ 0.43975541  0.43395001  0.4236806   0.50180626  0.4615185 ]

In [19]:
```

In machine learning, we often call these transformations **activation functions**. We usually combine weighted sums of inputs into them. When you consider the inputs, weights, and activation functions, that is called a **neuron** because it's inspired by biological neurons.

The details of how real neurons work in a physical brain is beyond the scope of this book. If you're interested in that, a neurobiology text might contain more, or you can take a look at Gordon M. Shepherd's *Foundation of the Neuron Doctrine* as one recent reference. Let's look at a simple example in TensorFlow:

```
w1 = tf.constant(0.1)
w2 = tf.constant(0.2)
sess.run(tf.global_variables_initializer())
```

First, just create some constants, w1 and w2. We'll multiply x1 by w1 and x2 by w2, then we will add these intermediate values, and finally put the result through a sigmoid activation function with tf.sigmoid. Take a look at the result shown in the following screenshot:

```
In [24]: print((w1*x1).eval())
[ 0.25280735  0.23198548  0.32570502  0.32763374  0.29772624]

In [25]: print((w2*x2).eval())
[-0.16239884 -0.26094452 -0.24706605 -0.228054   -0.14377597]

In [26]: print(n1.eval())
[ 0.52258676  0.49276075  0.51964962  0.52487439  0.53841174]

In [27]:
```

Again, don't worry about the exact formula right now, you can have a variety of different activation functions. Just note that this is your first step toward your own neural network.

So, how do we go from a single neuron to a whole network? Easy! The input of one neuron just becomes the input for another neuron in the next layer of the network.

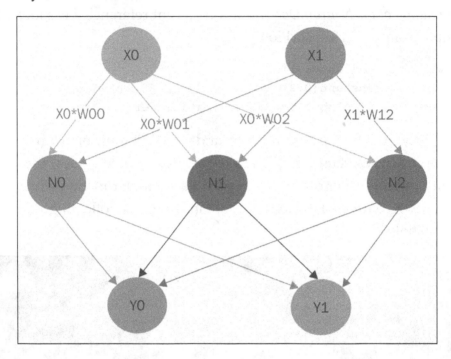

In the preceding diagram, we have a simple network with two inputs, **X0** and **X1**, two outputs, **Y0** and **Y1**, and three neurons in the middle. The value in **X0** gets sent to each of the *N* neurons, but there's a different weight, which is multiplied with the **X0** associated with each. **X1** is also sent to each neuron and has its own set of weights. For each neuron, we compute the weighted sum of inputs, put this through the activation function, and produce an intermediate output. Now, we do the same thing, but consider the outputs of the neurons to be the inputs of Ys. Note that, by taking nonlinear activations of weighted sums of inputs, we effectively just compute a new set of features for our eventual model.

Now you have learned the basics of nonlinear transformations in TensorFlow and what neural networks are. Well, they may not let you read minds, they are crucial for deep learning. In the next section, we'll use the simple neural network to improve our classification algorithm.

Single hidden layer model

Here, we'll put the basics of neural network into practice. We'll adapt the logistic regression TenserFlow code into a single hidden layer of neurons. Then, you'll learn the idea behind backpropagation to compute the weights, that is, train the net. Finally, you'll train your first true neural network in TensorFlow.

The TensorFlow code for this section should look familiar. It's just a slightly evolved version of the logistic regression code. Let's look at how to add a hidden layer of neurons that will compute nonlinear combinations of our input pixels.

You should start with a fresh Python session, execute the code to read in, and set up the data as in the logistic model. It's the same code, just copied to the new file:

```
import tensorflow as tf
import numpy as np
import math
from tqdm import tqdm
%autoindent
try:
    from tqdm import tqdm
except ImportError:
    def tqdm(x, *args, **kwargs):
        return x
```

You can always go back to the previous sections and remind yourself what that code does; everything up to the `num_hidden` variable will get you up to speed.

Exploring the single hidden layer model

Let's now explore the single hidden layer model in a step-by-step process:

1. First, let's specify how many neurons we want with `num_hidden = 128`; this is essentially how many nonlinear combinations will get passed to the logistic progression in the end.

2. To accommodate this, we also need to update the shape of the `W1` and `b1` weight tensors. They're now feeding into our hidden neurons, so they need to match the shape:

    ```
    W1 = tf.Variable(tf.truncated_normal([1296, num_hidden],
                                      stddev=1./math.sqrt(1296)))
    b1 = tf.Variable(tf.constant(0.1,shape=[num_hidden]))
    ```

3. The way we compute the activation function of the weighted sum is with the single `h1` line; this is to multiply our input pixels by their respective weights for each neuron:

    ```
    h1 = tf.sigmoid(tf.matmul(x,W1) + b1)
    ```

Add the neuron bias term, and finally, put this through the `sigmoid` activation function; at this point, we have 128 intermediate values:

```
In [23]: num_hidden = 128

In [24]: W1 = tf.Variable(tf.truncated_normal([1296, num_hidden],
   ....:                                       stddev=1./math.sqrt(1296)))

In [25]: b1 = tf.Variable(tf.constant(0.1,shape=[num_hidden]))

In [26]: h1 = tf.sigmoid(tf.matmul(x,W1) + b1)

In [27]:
```

4. Now it's just your friendly logistic regression again; you already know what to do. These newly computed 128 features need their own set of weights and biases to compute a score on the output class, that's `W2` and `b2`, respectively. Note how the shape matches the shape of the neurons 128, and the number of the output class is `5`:

```
W2 = tf.Variable(tf.truncated_normal([num_hidden, 5],

                                     stddev=1./math.sqrt(5)))
b2 = tf.Variable(tf.constant(0.1,shape=[5]))
sess.run(tf.global_variables_initializer())
```

In all these weights, we initialize them with this strange truncated normal call. With neural networks, we want to get a good spread of initial values so our weights can climb to meaningful values rather than just getting zeroed out.

5. Truncated normal holds random values from a normal distribution with the given standard deviation, a research standard scaled to the number of inputs, but throws out values that are too extreme, hence the truncation part of this. With our weights and neurons all defined, we set the final `softmax` model just as we did before, except we need to take care to use our 128 neurons as the input, `h1`, and the associated weights and biases, `W2` and `b2`:

```
y = tf.nn.softmax(tf.matmul(h1,W2) + b2)
```

Backpropagation

The key to training the weights of a neural network and many other machine learning models is called **backpropagation**.

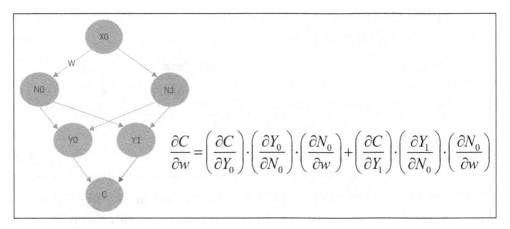

$$\frac{\partial C}{\partial w} = \left(\frac{\partial C}{\partial Y_0}\right)\cdot\left(\frac{\partial Y_0}{\partial N_0}\right)\cdot\left(\frac{\partial N_0}{\partial w}\right) + \left(\frac{\partial C}{\partial Y_1}\right)\cdot\left(\frac{\partial Y_1}{\partial N_0}\right)\cdot\left(\frac{\partial N_0}{\partial w}\right)$$

A full derivation is beyond the scope of this book, but let's go through it intuitively. When you train a model such as logistic regression in air and your training set comes directly from poorly chosen weights, you can see which weights should be adjusted and by how much and change them accordingly.

Formally, TensorFlow does this by computing the derivative of the air with respect to the weight and adjusting the weight by a fraction of this. Backpropagation is really an extension of the same process.

You start at the bottom output or cost function layer, computing derivatives, and use those to compute associated derivatives with neurons one layer up. We can compute the appropriate partial derivative of the cost with respect to the weight we want to adjust by adding up the product of the derivatives on the path from the cost up to the weight. The formula shown in the preceding diagram just spells out what the red arrows show. If this seems complicated, don't worry.

TensorFlow handles it for you behind the scenes with the optimizer. Because we carefully specified our model using TensorFlow to train it almost exactly the same as before, we'll use the same code here:

```
epochs = 5000
train_acc = np.zeros(epochs//10)
test_acc = np.zeros(epochs//10)
for i in tqdm(range(epochs), ascii=True):
    if i % 10 == 0: # Record summary data, and the accuracy
        # Check accuracy on train set
        A = accuracy.eval(feed_dict={x: train.
reshape([-1,1296]), y_: onehot_train})
        train_acc[i//10] = A

        # And now the validation set
        A = accuracy.eval(feed_dict={x: test.
reshape([-1,1296]), y_: onehot_test})
        test_acc[i//10] = A
    train_step.run(feed_dict={x: train.reshape([-1,1296]),
y_: onehot_train})
```

One thing to note is that, because we have these hidden neurons, there are many more weights to fit the model. This means that our model will take longer to run and that it has to take more iterations to train. Let's run it through 5000 epochs this time:

```
In [42]: epochs = 5000

In [43]: train_acc = np.zeros(epochs//10)

In [44]: test_acc = np.zeros(epochs//10)

In [45]: for i in tqdm(range(epochs), ascii = True):
    ....:     # Record summary data, and the accuracy
    ....:     if i % 10 == 0:
    ....:         # Check accuracy on train set
    ....:         A = accuracy.eval(feed_dict={
    ....:             x: train.reshape([-1,1296]),
    ....:             y_: onehot_train})
    ....:         train_acc[i//10] = A
    ....:         # And now the validation set
    ....:         A = accuracy.eval(feed_dict={
    ....:             x: test.reshape([-1,1296]),
    ....:             y_: onehot_test})
    ....:         test_acc[i//10] = A
    ....:     train_step.run(feed_dict={
    ....:         x: train.reshape([-1,1296]),
    ....:         y_: onehot_train})
```

This model probably takes longer than the previous one, maybe four times as long. So you can expect a few minutes to 10 minutes, depending on your computer. With the model training now, we'll look at verifying the accuracy later.

Single hidden layer explained

In this section, we'll carefully look at the model we built. First, we'll verify the overall accuracy of our model, then we'll see where the model goes wrong. Finally, we'll visualize the weights associated with several neurons to see what they're looking for:

```
plt.figure(figsize=(6, 6))
plt.plot(train_acc,'bo')
plt.plot(test_acc,'rx')
```

Make sure that you've trained your model as we did in the previous section, if not, you might want to stop here and do that first. Because we evaluated our model accuracy every 10 training epochs and saved the result, it's now easy to explore how our model has evolved.

Using Matplotlib, we can plot both the training accuracy (the blue dots) and testing accuracy (the red dots) on the same figure:

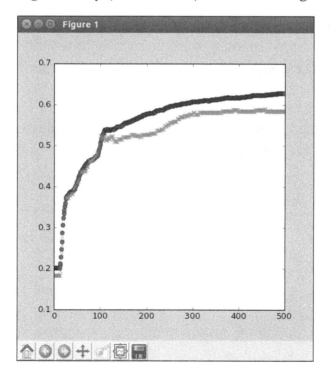

Again, if you don't have Matplotlib, that's okay. You can just look at the array values themselves. Note that the training accuracy (blue in color) is usually a little better than the testing accuracy (red in color). This isn't surprising, since the test images are totally new to the model and may contain previously unseen features. Also, observe how the accuracy generally climbs over more epochs, moving up, first quite a bit, and then slowly advancing. Our model here achieves about 60 percent accuracy; not perfect, but an improvement on the simple logistic regression.

To see where our model is getting mixed up, it's helpful to create the confusion matrix. That is, we'll look for an actual plot class, of one say; what did the model classify it as? Formally, a 5x5 matrix. For each testing image, we increment the value and position $i\,j$, if the image was actually class i and the model predicted class j. Note that, when the model gets this correct, then $i = j$.

A good model will have big values on the diagonal and not much elsewhere. This type of analysis makes it easy to see if two classes are often confused for each other or if some classes are rarely chosen by the model.

In the following example, we create the predicting classes by evaluating y, the class probabilities:

```
pred = np.argmax(y.eval(feed_dict={x:
    test.reshape([-1,1296]), y_: onehot_test}), axis = 1)
conf = np.zeros([5,5])
for p,t in zip(pred,np.argmax(onehot_test,axis=1)):
    conf[t,p] += 1

plt.matshow(conf)
plt.colorbar()
```

The np.argmax function extracts the position with the largest probability. Similarly, to determine the actual class, we use np.argmax to undo the one-hot encoding. Creating the confusion matrix starts with an all-zero array and we step through the testing data filling it in. Matplotlib lets us look at a color image, but printing the conferee is nearly as effective:

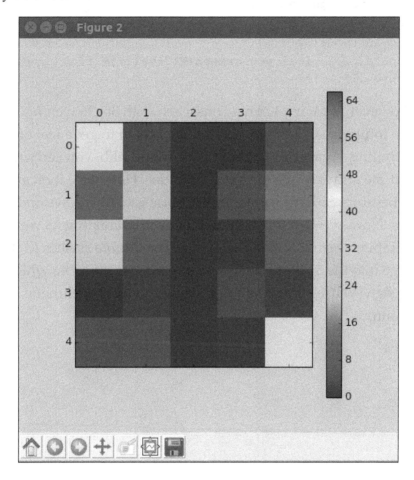

In the preceding output, we see that the model generally does a decent job, except that it rarely predicts class 2. Your exact results may look a little different because of initial randomness.

Understanding weights of the model

Just as we view the weights for our logistic regression model, we can spy on the weights for this model:

```
plt.figure(figsize=(6, 6))
f, plts = plt.subplots(4,8, sharex=True)
for i in range(32):
    plts[i//8, i%8].pcolormesh(W1.eval()[:,i].
reshape([36,36]))
```

Now, however, we have 128 neurons, each with 36x36 weights coming from the input pixels. Let's look at a few of them to get a feel of what they're finding. Again, if you don't have Matplotlib, you can simply print out the arrays to see the same behavior. Here we'll look at 32 of the 128 neurons. So, let's format our subplot into four rows and eight columns. Now, we step through each neuron evaluating its weight and reshaping them into the image size. The double slashes (//) put the image into the appropriate row using integer division, while the percent sign (%) uses the remainder, really modular arithmetic, to pick the column.

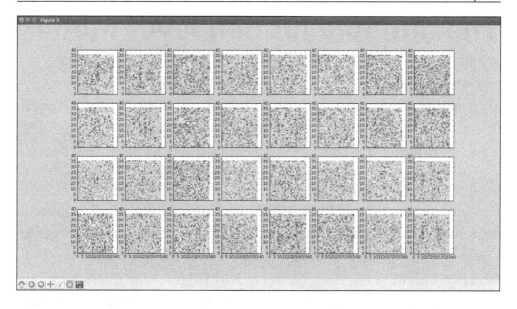

Visually, in the preceding output, you can see some shapes sticking out. Some neurons have more or less a circular shape compared to their weight patterns. Others look random, but might be picking up features that we can't easily intuit. We can try to visualize the weights of the output layer as well, but these are no longer intuitive. We call that because of our neural network. The output logistic regression is now 128 input values, along with weights being used to compute 5 scores. There's no longer an image structure, since every pixel went into every neuron on the hidden layer. Now you know how to assess and interpret neural network results. Good job!

The multiple hidden layer model

In this section, we'll show you how to build even more complex models with additional hidden layers. We'll adapt our single hidden layer model into a multilayer model known as a **deep neural network**. Then, we'll discuss choosing how many neurons and layers to use. Finally, we'll train the model itself, being patient, as this might take a while to compute.

Remember when we added a hidden layer of neurons to our logistic regression model? Well, we can do that again, adding another layer to our single hidden layer model. Once you have more than one layer of neurons, we call this a deep neural network. However, everything you learned before can be applied now. As in the previous sections of this chapter, you should make a fresh Python session and execute the code up to `num_hidden1` in this section's code file. Then the fun starts.

```python
In [2]:

import tensorflow as tf
import numpy as np
import math
%autoindent
try:
    from tqdm import tqdm
except ImportError:
    def tqdm(x, *args, **kwargs):
        return x


# Load data
data = np.load('data_with_labels.npz')
train = data['arr_0']/255.
labels = data['arr_1']

# Look at some data
print(train[0])
print(labels[0])

# If you have matplotlib installed
import matplotlib.pyplot as plt
plt.ion()

def to_onehot(labels,nclasses = 5):
    '''
    Convert labels to "one-hot" format.

    >>> a = [0,1,2,3]
    >>> to_onehot(a,5)
    array([[ 1.,  0.,  0.,  0.,  0.],
           [ 0.,  1.,  0.,  0.,  0.],
           [ 0.,  0.,  1.,  0.,  0.],
           [ 0.,  0.,  0.,  1.,  0.]])
    '''
```

Exploring the multiple hidden layer model

Let's start by changing the old `num_hidden` to `num_hidden1` to indicate the number of neurons on the first hidden layer:

```
# Hidden layer 1
num_hidden1 = 128
```

Be sure to change the variables, defining the weight and bias variables as well. Now we'll insert our second hidden layer:

```
W1 = tf.Variable(tf.truncated_normal([1296,num_hidden1],
                          stddev=1./math.sqrt(1296)))
b1 = tf.Variable(tf.constant(0.1,shape=[num_hidden1]))
h1 = tf.sigmoid(tf.matmul(x,W1) + b1)
```

Let's use the one with `32` neurons this time. Note how the shape of the weights must account for every one of the 128 intermediate outputs from the previous layer coming into the 32 inputs or neurons of the current layer, but we initialize our weights and biases essentially the same way:

```
# Hidden Layer 2
num_hidden2 = 32
W2 = tf.Variable(tf.truncated_normal([num_hidden1,
             num_hidden2],stddev=2./math.sqrt(num_hidden1)))
b2 = tf.Variable(tf.constant(0.2,shape=[num_hidden2]))
h2 = tf.sigmoid(tf.matmul(h1,W2) + b2)
```

As you can see in the preceding code, we create the `h2` output with a `sigmoid` function, as we did before, with a matrix multiply, addition, and function call.

For the output logistic regression layer, we just need to update the variable names:

```
# Output Layer
W3 = tf.Variable(tf.truncated_normal([num_hidden2, 5],
                                    stddev=1./math.sqrt(5)))
b3 = tf.Variable(tf.constant(0.1,shape=[5]))
```

These are now the third set of weights, and of course, this shape must match the output of the preceding hidden layer, so, 32 by 5:

```
In [30]: W3 = tf.Variable(tf.truncated_normal([num_hidden2, 5],
   ....:                                     stddev=1./math.sqrt(5)))

In [31]: b3 = tf.Variable(tf.constant(0.1,shape=[5]))

In [32]: sess.run(tf.global_variables_initializer())

In [33]: y = tf.nn.softmax(tf.matmul(h2,W3) + b3)

In [34]:
```

Don't forget to update the y model function with the h2, W3, and b3 variables. You wouldn't want to update all the code, only to use an old model.

You might be wondering how we decided on 128 neurons for the first layer and 32 neurons for the second layer. The truth is that determining a good size and shape for your network can be a challenging problem. Though it may be computationally expensive, trial and error is one way to develop the model. Typically, you might start with an old model and work from there. Here, we started with a single hidden layer of 128 neurons and tried adding a new layer underneath. We want to compute some features to discriminate five classes, so we should keep that in mind when picking the number of neurons.

Generally, it's better to start small and work your way up to a minimal model that explains the data. If a model with 128 neurons on the top layer and 8 neurons on the next layer does poorly, this may indicate that we need more features for the final layer and should add more neurons, not fewer.

Try doubling the number of neurons in the final layer, and of course, it's good to go back to earlier layers and tweak the number of neurons there too. Likewise, you can change the learning rate of the optimizer, which changes how much the weights get adjusted in every step, and even change the function used for optimizing.

> Setting all these values is called **hyperparameter optimization**, a hot topic in machine learning research.

Note that we're essentially starting from the simplest possible model, logistic regression, and slowly adding on new features and structures. If a simple model works well, it may not even be necessary to spend time on something more advanced.

Now that our model is specified, let's actually train it:

```
# Climb on cross-entropy
cross_entropy = tf.reduce_mean(
    tf.nn.softmax_cross_entropy_with_logits(logits= y +
1e-50, labels= y_))

# How we train
train_step = tf.train.GradientDescentOptimizer(0.01).
minimize(cross_entropy)

# Define accuracy
correct_prediction = tf.equal(tf.argmax(y,1),tf.
argmax(y_,1))
accuracy=tf.reduce_mean(tf.cast(correct_prediction,
"float"))
```

Again, we need to redefine our training nodes in the TensorFlow graph, but these are exactly the same as before. Note that, because our first hidden layer now hooks into another layer of neurons, we have many more weights to compute. The following is the actual training code:

```
epochs = 25000
train_acc = np.zeros(epochs//10)
test_acc = np.zeros(epochs//10)
for i in tqdm(range(epochs)):
    # Record summary data, and the accuracy
    if i % 10 == 0:
        # Check accuracy on train set
        A = accuracy.eval(feed_dict={
            x: train.reshape([-1,1296]),
            y_: onehot_train})
        train_acc[i//10] = A
        # And now the validation set
        A = accuracy.eval(feed_dict={
            x: test.reshape([-1,1296]),
            y_: onehot_test})
        test_acc[i//10] = A
    train_step.run(feed_dict={
        x: train.reshape([-1,1296]),
        y_: onehot_train})
```

Before, we had 128 times 5 weights, but now we have 128 times 32 weights — over six times as much for this layer, and this is on top of the initial weights from pixels to the first layer of neurons. One downside of deep neural networks is that they can take a while to train. Here, we'll run for 25000 epochs to ensure that the weights converge:

```
In [38]: epochs = 25000

In [39]: train_acc = np.zeros(epochs//10)

In [40]: test_acc = np.zeros(epochs//10)

In [41]: for i in tqdm(range(epochs), ascii = True):
             # Record summary data, and the accuracy
             if i % 10 == 0:
                 # Check accuracy on train set
                 A = accuracy.eval(feed_dict={
                     x: train.reshape([-1,1296]),
                     y_: onehot_train})
                 train_acc[i//10] = A
                 # And now the validation set
                 A = accuracy.eval(feed_dict={
                     x: test.reshape([-1,1296]),
                     y_: onehot_test})
                 test_acc[i//10] = A
             train_step.run(feed_dict={
                 x: train.reshape([-1,1296]),
                 y_: onehot_train})
```

This may take an hour or longer depending on your computer and GPU. While this might seem excessive, professional machine learning researchers often train models for up to two weeks. You might learn quickly, but the computer takes a while.

In this section, we have built and trained a truly deep neural network using TensorFlow. Many professional machine learning models are less complicated than what you've written already.

Results of the multiple hidden layer

Now, we'll look into what's going on inside a deep neural network. First, we'll verify the model accuracy. Then, we'll visualize and study the pixel weights. Finally, we'll look at the output weights as well.

After you've trained your deep neural network, let's take a look at the model accuracy. We'll do this the same way that we did for the single hidden layer model. The only difference this time, is that we have many more saved samples of the training and testing accuracy, having gone from many more epochs.

As always, don't worry if you don't have Matplotlib; printing parts of the arrays is fine.

Understanding the multiple hidden layers graph

Execute the following code to see the result:

```
# Plot the accuracy curves
plt.figure(figsize=(6,6))
plt.plot(train_acc,'bo')
plt.plot(test_acc,'rx')
```

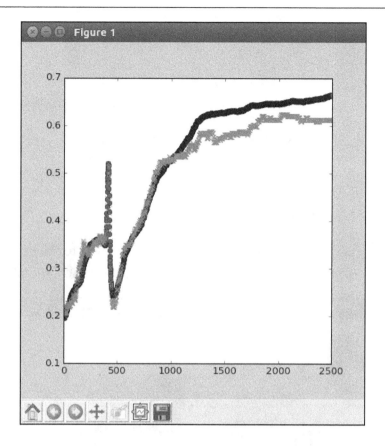

From the preceding output graph, we reach about 68 percent training accuracy and maybe 63 percent validation accuracy. This isn't too bad, but it does leave room for some improvement.

Let's take a moment to look at how the accuracy grows over many epochs. Of course, it starts terribly and it has some initial troubles, but the weights are random and still learning at that point, and it quickly improves over the first several thousand epochs. While it may get stuck in local maxima for a time, it usually climbs out and eventually slows its accent. Note that it still climbs well into the training period; it's only near the end here that the model may have reached its full capacity. Your curves might look a little different based on random initialization, but that's okay; it's your model and it's pretty good.

To see where our model is having trouble, let's look at the confusion matrix:

```
pred = np.argmax(y.eval(feed_dict={x:
    test.reshape([-1,1296]), y_: onehot_test}), axis = 1)
conf = np.zeros([5,5])
for p,t in zip(pred,np.argmax(onehot_test,axis=1)):
    conf[t,p] += 1

plt.matshow(conf)
plt.colorbar()
```

Again, this is exactly the same process that we used for the single hidden layer model, just on something a little more advanced:

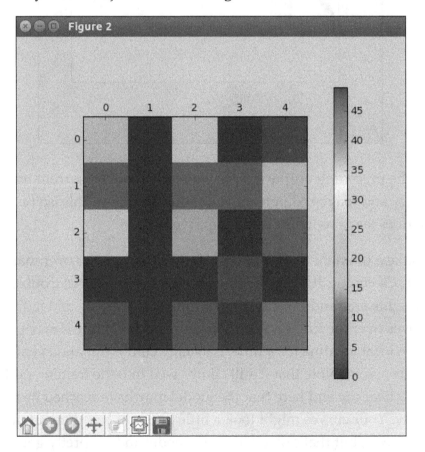

Plotting this, we see, as in the preceding output, that the model is doing well overall, but still has trouble identifying one of the classes, this time class 1; we're making incremental progress. With the accuracy verified, let's check out what kind of phenomena our first layer of neurons, those 128 guys, are finding:

```
# Let's look at a subplot of some weights
f, plts = plt.subplots(4,8, sharex=True)
for i in range(32):
    plts[i//8, i%8].matshow(W1.eval()[:,i].
reshape([36,36]))
```

For simplicity, we'll only look at the first 32 such neurons. Using the same code from the previous model, these are easy to plot with Matplotlib, or to print out:

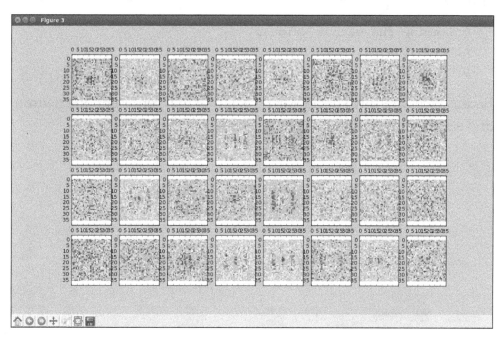

Not surprisingly, we saw many of the same kinds of features as in the previous model; although, here, they're going to be in different positions, even if it looks like the same type of feature, again, due to the random initializations. Again, you have some circular-type neurons, neurons that find very stripy features, and another neuron that finds sort of broad stripes. As far as our neural network is concerned, circular shapes and stripy shapes are good ingredients for determining font class.

While the weights in our other hidden layers no longer have the structure of an image, it can be instructive to look at the weights of the output. This will tell us how much each final neuron contributes to each class. We can plot this as one heat map or print a single array either way using W3.eval:

```
# Examine the output weights
plt.matshow(W3.eval())
plt.colorbar()
```

Because we carefully specified W3, each row will represent one neuron and each column will represent one class:

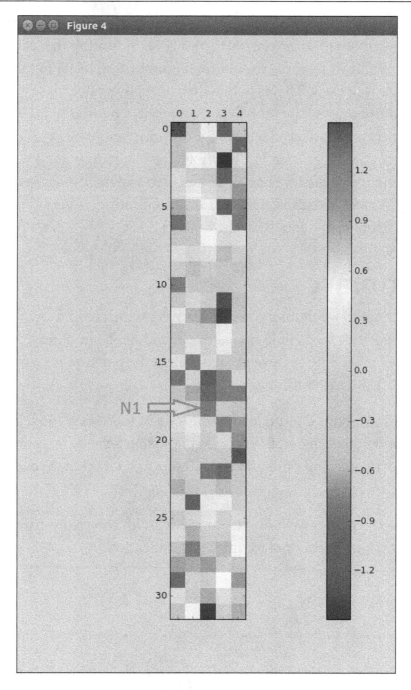

We can see from the preceding output graph that different neurons contribute more to some classes than others, indicating that certain overall nonlinear features the neuron is computing relate to that particular font class. That is, while the values these neurons produce are used to compute the scores for every font, a neuron that's very important and has a large weight for one font, might be nearly irrelevant in another font. For example, the **N1** neuron has a very large weight for class 2, but has almost zero weight for all the other classes. Whatever feature this neuron is computing, is very important to class 2, but not so much for the other classes.

Summary

In this chapter, we embraced deep learning with TensorFlow. Though we started with the simple model of one hidden layer of neurons, it didn't take you long to develop and train a deep neural network for the font classification problem.

You learned about the single and multiple hidden layer model and understood those in detail. You also understand the different types of neural networks and built and trained our first neural network with TensorFlow.

In the next chapter, we'll prove our model with convolutional neural networks, a powerful tool for image classification.

3
Convolutional Neural Networks

In the previous chapter we explored deep neural networks, which required ever more parameters to fit. This chapter will guide you through one of the most powerful developments in deep learning and let us use some of our knowledge about the problem space to improve the model. First we're going to explain what a convolutional layer is in a neural net followed by a TensorFlow example. Then we'll do the same for what's called a pooling layer. Finally, we'll adapt our font classification model into a **Convolutional Neural Network (CNN)** and see how it does.

In this chapter, we will look at the background of convolutional neural nets. We will also implement a convolutional layer in TensorFlow. We will learn max pooling layers and put them into practice and implement a single pooling layer as an example.

At the end of this chapter, you will have great control over the following concepts:

- Convolutional layer motivation
- Convolutional layer application

- Pooling layer motivation
- Pooling layer application
- Deep CNN
- Deeper CNN
- Wrapping up Deep CNN

Now let's jump into just what a convolutional layer is.

Convolutional layer motivation

In this section, we're going to walk through using a convolutional layer on an example image. We'll graphically see how convolution is just a sliding window. Further we'll learn how to extract multiple features from a window as well as accept multiple layers of input to a window.

In a classic dense layer of a neural network for a given neuron every input feature gets its own weight.

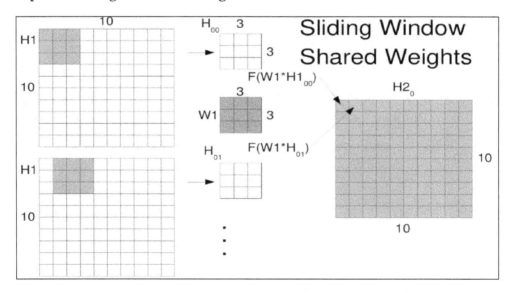

This is great if the input features are totally independent and measure different things, but what if there is structure among your features. The easiest example to imagine this happening is if your input features are pixels from an image. Some pixels are next to each other, others are far away.

For a task like image classification, and font classification especially, it often doesn't matter where a small scale feature occurs in an image. We can look for small scale features in a larger image by sliding a smaller window throughout the image, and this is key to using the same weight matrix no matter where in the image this window is positioned. In this way we can always look for the same feature anywhere.

Suppose we have a 10x10 image and we want to slide a 3x3 window through it. Typically machine learning engineers will slide this window by just one pixel at a time. This is called the **stride** so there is some overlap from one window to the next. Then element-wise multiply our small 3x3 weight matrix **W1** into our window $\mathbf{H1}_{00}$, sum the results, and put it through an activation function called **F**.

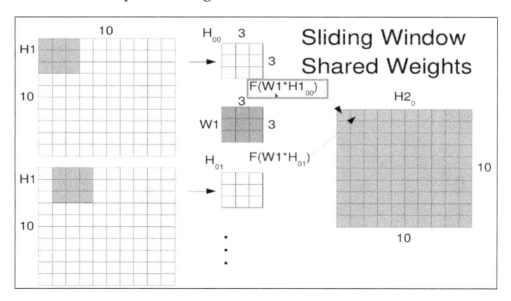

The first window **W1** goes into the first position of a new matrix shown as **H2** on the right. The window slides over one using the same weights but the result occupies position two. Note that we're essentially using the upper-left pixel as the reference point for where we store the result. Slide your window around the whole input image to generate the convolutional output. The dots in the following image are just a reminder that you'll be sliding this window around the whole space not just the two positions shown in the image:

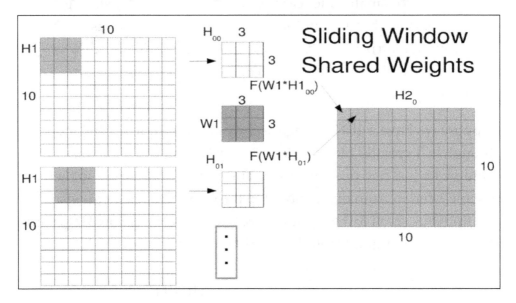

You might be wondering what happens when a window reaches the edge of the image. The choice is essentially to go between ignoring windows that go over the edge and padding them out with placeholder values. For convolutional layers the common choice is to pad them out often with zeros or an average value. This is called **same padding** in Tensorflow so called because the output shape of your convolution remains the same.

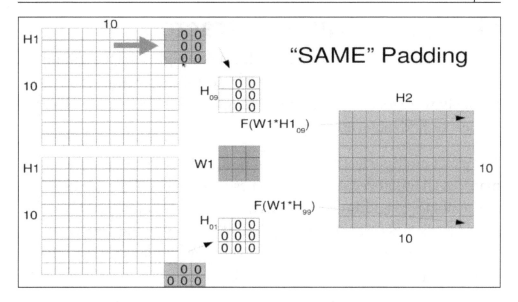

Note that in your final window this is only really looking at one value. But that pixel took part in many other positions so don't feel like it's been left out.

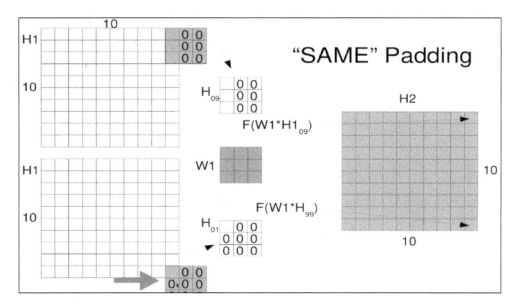

Multiple features extracted

The previous section featured a single set of weights for the sliding window. This essentially lets you compute a sliding feature. But you probably want to look for multiple things in the same window like a vertical or horizontal edge maybe.

To extract multiple features you just need to have additional weight matrices all initialized differently. These multiple sets of weights are analogies to additional neurons and a densely connected layer. Each matrix of weights **W1** (blue) and **W2** (green) in the center will gain you another matrix of output for additional hues shown in the following diagram as **H2**$_1$ (pink) and **H2**$_0$ (orange) on the right.

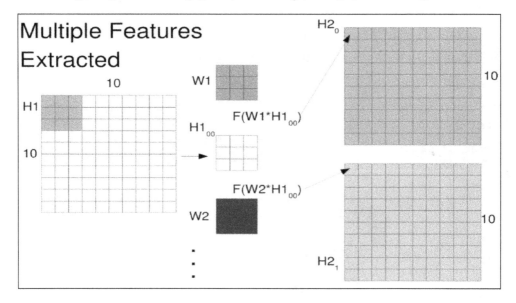

Just as you can pull multiple features out of a convolution you can put multiple features into such a network. The most obvious example is an image with multiple colors.

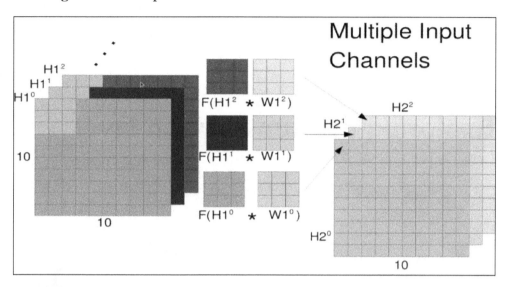

Now, observe the matrixes shown in the preceding diagram. You really have a matrix with red values, a matrix with green values, and a matrix with blue values. Your weight matrix is really now a weight tensor of size 3x3x3 with a window of the same size across the colors. Of course, you can combine all these approaches and this is typically done especially after your first convolutional layer when you've computed, say, 32 features on the window; now you have many input channels for the next layer.

Convolutional layer application

Now let's implement a simple convolutional layer in TensorFlow. First, we're going to go over the explicit shapes used in this example, as that's often tricky. Then we'll walk through the implementation and TensorFlow call for convolutions. Finally, we'll visually inspect the results of our convolution by passing in a simple example image.

Exploring the convolution layer

Let's jump right into the code with a fresh IPython session.

```
import tensorflow as tf
import math
import numpy as np

sess = tf.InteractiveSession()

# Make some fake data, 1 data points
image = np.random.randint(10,size=[1,10,10]) + np.eye(10)*10

# TensorFlow placeholder
# None is for batch processing
# (-1 keeps same size)
# 10x10 is the shape
# 1 is the number of "channels"
# (like RGB colors or gray)
x = tf.placeholder("float", [None, 10, 10])
x_im = tf.reshape(x, [-1,10,10,1])

### Convolutional Layer

# Window size to use, 3x3 here
winx = 3
winy = 3

# How many features to compute on the window
num_filters = 2

# Weight shape should match window size
# The '1' represents the number of
# input "channels" (colors)
W1 = tf.Variable(tf.truncated_normal(
    [winx, winy,1, num_filters],
    stddev=1./math.sqrt(winx*winy)))
b1 = tf.Variable(tf.constant(
    0.1,shape=[num_filters]))
```

This is just a small example to help us get familiar with using TensorFlow for convolution layers.

After importing the necessary tools, let's make a fake 10x10 image but with larger values on the diagonal:

```
# Make some fake data, 1 data points
image = np.random.randint(10,size=[1,10,10]) +
np.eye(10)*10
```

Note the unusual size specified in the preceding code. The `10, 10` is just the image dimensions but the `1` refers to the number of input channels. In this case, we're using one input channel, which is like a gray scale image. If you had a color image, this might be three channels to represent red, green, and blue colors.

Though the example here and the research problem only have one channel, gray-scale, we'll see in the *Deep CNN* section how producing multiple inputs from a convolution layer leads to a multichannel input in the next convolution layer. So you'll still get a feel with how to handle that.

Moving down to the TensorFlow place holder, we also do something that might seem unusual.

```
x = tf.placeholder("float", [None, 10, 10])
x_im = tf.reshape(x, [-1,10,10,1])
```

Right after writing the placeholder variable in a natural way with `10, 10` and `None` for the possible batch processing of many images, we call `tf.reshape`. This is to rearrange the dimensions of our image, and get them in a shape TensorFlow expects. The `-1` just means to fill out the dimensions as needed to maintain the overall size. The `10,10` is, of course, our image dimension, and the final `1`, is now the number of channels. Again, if you had a color image with three channels, this would be a three.

For our convolutional layer example, we want to look at windows of the image that are three pixels tall and three pixels wide. So we specify those as shown in the following code:

```
# Window size to use, 3x3 here
winx = 3
winy = 3
```

Also, let's extract two features from each window so that's our number of filters:

```
# How many features to compute on the window
num_filters = 2
```

You might also see this called the number of kernels.

Specifying the weight is where things get really interesting but it's not hard once you know the syntax.

```
W1 = tf.Variable(tf.truncated_normal(
    [winx, winy,1, num_filters],
    stddev=1./math.sqrt(winx*winy)))
```

We're using `tf.truncated_normal` as we did earlier to generate random weights. But the size is very peculiar. The attributes, `winx` and `winy` are, of course, the dimensions of our window, `1` here is the number of input channels, so just gray-scale, and the final dimension (`num_filters`) is the output dimension, the number of filters.

Again, this is an analogy to the number of neurons for a densely connected layer. For the standard deviation on the randomness, we still scale to the number of parameters, but note that we have a parameter for each weight, so `win x*win y`.

And the bias of course needs a variable for each output neuron, so one for each filter:

```
b1 = tf.Variable(tf.constant(
    0.1,shape=[num_filters]))
```

The `tf.nn.conv2d` function is really the heart of the operation here. We first pass in our reshaped input `x_im`, then the weights that are applied to every window, and then the `strides` argument.

 The `strides` argument tells TensorFlow how much to move your window by at every step.

Typical usage for convolution layers, is the shift by one pixel to the right and when you finish a row, shift by one pixel down. So there's a great deal of overlap. If you want to shift by two pixels to the right, and two down; however, you could input `strides=[1,2,2,1]`. The last number is for moving over channels and the first is for moving over separate images in a batch. Setting these to 1, is the most common approach.

```
xw = tf.nn.conv2d(x_im, W1,
        strides=[1, 1, 1, 1],
        padding='SAME')
```

The `padding='SAME'` is exactly as described in the last section. This means that the sliding window will run even if part of it is beyond the bounds of your input image. Combined with a stride of one, this means that the convolutional output dimensions will be the same as the input, not counting the number of channels or filters of course.

Finally, we want to pass this convolutional output through an activation function:

```
h1 = tf.nn.relu(xw + b1)
```

Here we're using the `relu` function, which stands for rectified linear. Basically, this just means that any negative input gets set to zero while positive inputs stay the same. You'll see this activation used often with convolutional neural networks. So it's good to be familiar with it. Since we've already multiplied the `W1` weights, we just need to add the bias terms here to produce the convolutional layer output.

Initialize the variables in TensorFlow:

```
# Remember to initialize!
sess.run(tf.global_variables_initializer())
```

Now, you have a working convolution. Nice! Let's take a quick look at the fruits of our labor.

First, we need to evaluate the `h1` node, passing in our example image as the data:

```
# Peek inside
H = h1.eval(feed_dict = {x: image})
```

So we know where to start let's look at the example image using the following code:

```
# Let's take a look
import matplotlib.pyplot as plt
plt.ion()

# Original
plt.matshow(image[0])
plt.colorbar()
```

The 0 in the preceding code is just because of the strange shaping, there are not really multiple data points. You can see that the values on the diagonal are larger than the other values, just to be distinct from being purely random:

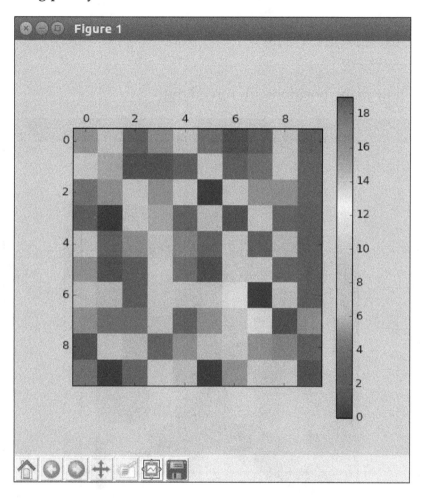

Let's take a look at the first output feature, recall that the output H has a shape of 1,10,10,2, because there's 1 data point, 10 pixels in width and height, and 2 features. So to grab the first, we want all the pixels and the zero with filter. Okay, that's interesting.

```
# Conv channel 1
plt.matshow(H[0,:,:,0])
plt.colorbar()
```

Notice how many positions are zeroed out:

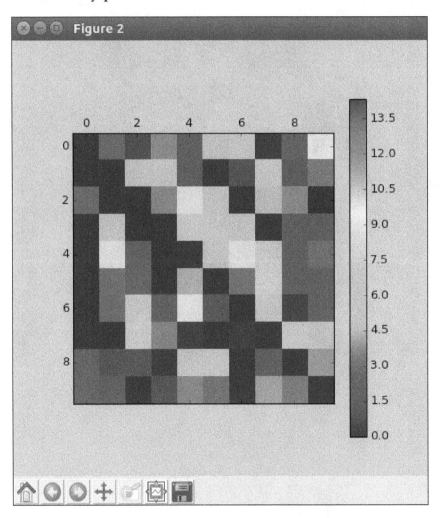

That's the rectify part of the `relu` activation. Neat. The second feature should look similar, up to random initialization. These weights haven't been trained on anything yet, so we shouldn't expect them to produce meaningful output. Here we see there happens to be many zeroes but otherwise, there are many small values.

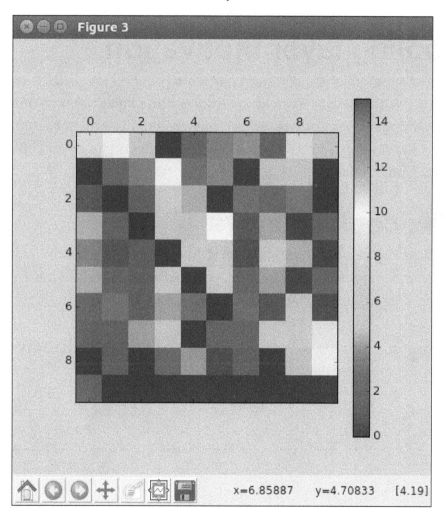

Your images might look more or less different, the important thing to note, is that our output dimensions are the same but it's like we have two different views of the same image. In this section, we created our first convolutional layer in TensorFlow mastering the odd shapes required.

Pooling layer motivation

Now let's understand a common partner to pooling layers. In this section, we're going to learn about max pooling layers being similar to convolutional layers, although they have some differences in common usage. We'll wrap up by showing how these layers can be combined for maximum effect.

Max pooling layers

Suppose you've used a convolutional layer to extract a feature from an image and suppose hypothetically, you had a small weight matrix that detects a dog shape in the window of the image.

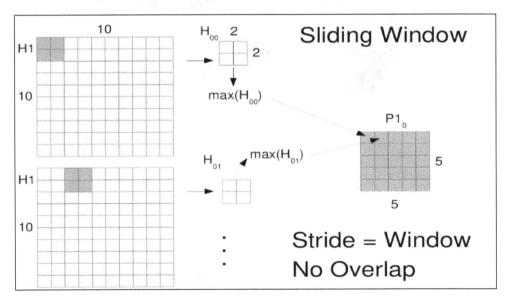

When you convolve this around your output is likely to report many nearby regions with dog shapes. But this is really just due to the overlap. There probably aren't many dogs all next to each other, though maybe an image of puppies would. You'd really only like to see that feature once and preferably wherever it is strongest. The max pooling layer attempts to do this. Like a convolutional layer a pooling layer works on a small sliding windows of an image.

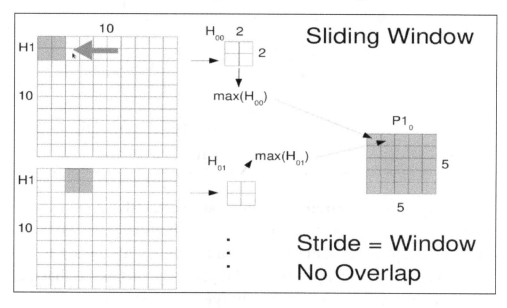

Typically, researchers add a pooling layer after one or more convolutional layers. You most often see them with window sizes of 2x2. All you do is extract the four adjacent values, here referring to H_{00} usually no weights are applied to them. Now, we want to combine these four values in a way to extract the most interesting feature of this window. Typically, we want to pull out the most striking feature, so we choose the pixel with the maximum value ($max(H_{00})$) and throw out the rest. But, you could also average the results or do something more exotic. Also, while our convolutional windows had a great deal of overlap, with pooling windows, we usually don't want any overlap, so this stride will equal window size 2.

In the preceding 10x10 example output, our pooling output is only 5x5 because of this change in stride.

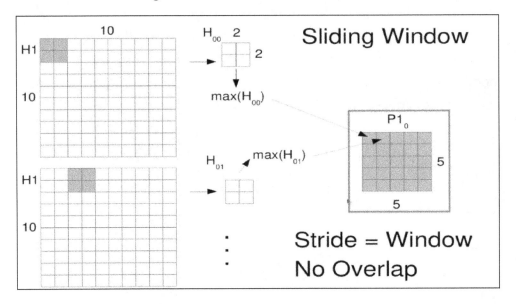

Another key difference from convolutional layers, is that pooling layers often use a different padding scheme, whereas convolutional layers are happy to use same padding and pad out with zeros, we most often use pooling layers with valid padding. This means that if a window is beyond the bounds of an image, we throw it out.

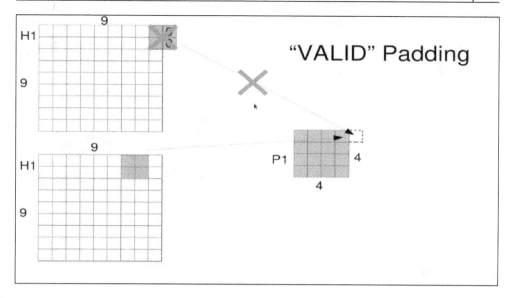

This does lose some information at the edges but ensures that outputs aren't being biased by padding values.

 Note that this example uses a 9x9 input to the pooling layer, but because of the valid padding and stride of 2, the output will only be 4x4. An 8x8 input would also have 4x4 output.

The real strength of convolutional and pooling layers comes when you combine them. Most often you'll see a convolutional layer at the top input side of a model, maybe with a 3x3 window.

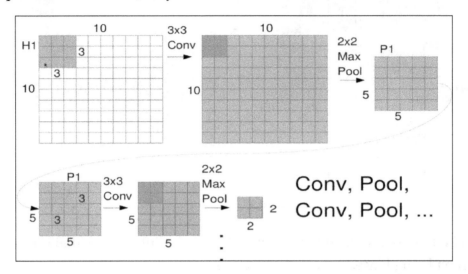

This looks for the same set of features anywhere in an image.

Then a 2x2 max pooling layer immediately follows, pooling out only the regions most exhibiting the features and cutting down the size. You can iterate this process too.

After pooling, you now have essentially a smaller image **P1** but instead of pixel color intensities, you have feature intensities. So you can create another convolutional layer to read in the output of the first pooling, that is the **P1** present at the bottom and then you can apply another max pooling layer to this. Note how because of the pooling, the image size is gradually shrinking. Intuitively, you can think of this as building up larger scale features that span larger regions of the image.

Early convolutional weights often train to detect simple edges and successive convolutional layers combine those edges into gradually more complex shapes such as faces, cars, and even dogs.

Pooling layer application

In this section, we're going to take a look at the TensorFlow function for max pooling, then we'll talk about transitioning from a pooling layer back to a fully connected layer. Finally, we'll visually look at the pooling output to verify its reduced size.

Let's pick up in our example from where we left off in the previous section. Make sure you've executed everything up to the pound pooling layer before starting this exercise.

Recall we've put a 10x10 image through a 3x3 convolution and rectified linear activation. Now, let's add a 2x2 max pooling layer that comes after our convolutional layer.

```
p1 = tf.nn.max_pool(h1, ksize=[1, 2, 2, 1],
        strides=[1, 2, 2, 1], padding='VALID')
```

The key to this is `tf.nn.max_pool`. The first argument is just the output of our previous convolutional layer, `h1`. Next we have the strange `ksize`. This really just defines the window size of our pooling. In this case, 2x2. The first `1` refers to how many data points to pull over at once or the batch. Typically we leave this as `1`. The final `1` refers to the number of channels to include in the pooling at once. Note that here we have two channels because the convolution produced two output filters. But we only have a `1` in this position; this is the only fault the max of a single feature at a time. Strides works just as it did in the convolution layer. The difference here is that we use 2x2, the size of our pooling window, because we don't want any overlap. The pre and post `1` values are exactly the same as in the convolutional layer.

So our output will be half the size in each dimension, here 5x5. Finally, we set the `padding` to `VALID`. This means that if a window were to go beyond the edge of the image, really the convolutional output, we would throw that out and not use it. If our pooling layer feeds into yet another convolutional layer, you can add that in the following code line:

```
# We automatically determine the size
p1_size = np.product([s.value for s in p1.get_shape()[1:]])
```

But what if you're done with convolutional layers and want to feed into a classic fully connected layer like in our model from the previous section. This is easy to do; we just need to flatten our output from a 2D matrix with many channels of output to a long, one-dimensional vector.

This line is one-way to automatically compute the length of the flattened pooling output. All it does is multiply the sizes of all the dimensions. So a 5x5 matrix with two channels would yield *5x5x2*, which is *50* outputs. The next line `tf.reshape` uses this value to actually flatten the array:

```
p1f = tf.reshape(p1, [-1, p1_size ])
```

The `-1` in the preceding code line is to handle potential batching of many input images at once. It tells TensorFlow to pick this first dimension such that the overall number of parameters remains the same. Let's peek at the output of our pooling layer so we can see a concrete example:

```
P = p1.eval(feed_dict = {x: image})
```

First we have to actually evaluate our pooling output given our input image.

Because the pooling layer depends on the convolutional layer, TensorFlow will automatically put our image through that first. We can look at the results the exact same way as we did for the convolutional output.

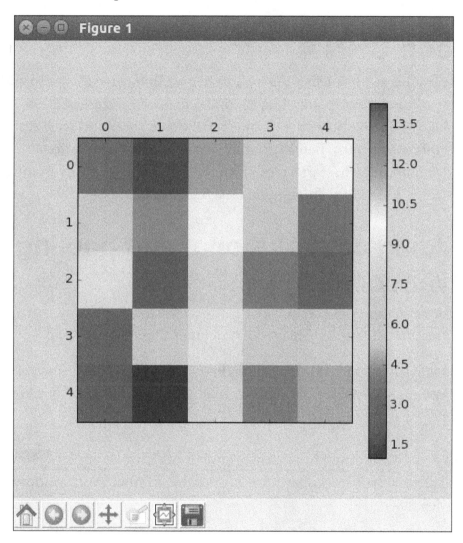

Just looking at the preceding first filter output, you can notice that it's 5x5.

Also note that the values present were all in some cell of the convolution output. Since our only activation on the pooling layer is the maximum, three values get dropped in each 2x2 window and one advances to the next layer.

Deep CNN

Now, in this section, let's think big. In this section, we're going to add a convolutional and pooling layer combo to our font classification model. We'll make sure to feed this into a dense layer and we'll see how this model does. Before jumping into the new convolutional model, make sure to start a fresh IPython session. Execute everything up to `num_filters = 4` and you'll be ready to go.

Adding convolutional and pooling layer combo

For our convolutional layer we're going to use a 5x5 window with four features extracted. This is a little bigger than the example.

We really want the model to learn something now. First we should use `tf.reshape` to put our 36x36 image into a tensor of size 36x36x1.

```
x_im = tf.reshape(x, [-1,36,36,1])
```

This is only important to keep the number of channels straight. Now we'll just set up the constants for our number of filters and window as just described:

```
num_filters = 4
winx = 5
winy = 5
```

We can set up our weight tensor just like we did in the example problem:

```
W1 = tf.Variable(tf.truncated_normal(
    [winx, winy, 1 , num_filters],
    stddev=1./math.sqrt(winx*winy)))
```

The `winx` and `winy` constants are just window dimensions. The `1` value is the number of input channels, just gray, and `num_filters` is how many features we're extracting. Again it's like the number of neurons in a dense layer. The bias works the same way but it only worries about the number of filters:

```
b1 = tf.Variable(tf.constant(0.1,
                shape=[num_filters]))
```

The call to `conv2d` itself is also the same as our example.

```
xw = tf.nn.conv2d(x_im, W1,
                strides=[1, 1, 1, 1],
                padding='SAME')
```

Good thing we generalized it there to make life easy now. Following is the description of the preceding code lines:

- `x_im` is transformed input
- `W1` attribute is the weight matrix we just specified
- `strides` tells TensorFlow to move the window by one each step
- `padding='SAME'` means to accept windows over the edge of the image

Now we can put our convolution through the `relu` activation function to complete the convolutional layer. Good job!

```
h1 = tf.nn.relu(xw + b1)
```

The pooling layer is also exactly the same as in the previous section:

```
# 2x2 Max pooling, no padding on edges
p1 = tf.nn.max_pool(h1, ksize=[1, 2, 2, 1],
        strides=[1, 2, 2, 1], padding='VALID')
```

Just to review we slide a 2x2 window, the `ksize`, over the convolutional output sliding by two each time the stride. When we would reach beyond the edge of the data the `padding='VALID'` tells us to stop. Now that we have a combined convolutional and pooling layer let's append a typical densely connected layer:

```
p1_size = np.product(
        [s.value for s in p1.get_shape()[1:]])
p1f = tf.reshape(p1, [-1, p1_size ])
```

First we need to reshape the pooling output to be a one-dimensional vector. This is exactly what we did in the last section. We automatically compute the dimensions of the pooling output to get the number of parameters for flattening.

CNN to classify our fonts

Now let's create a densely connected layer with 32 neurons:

```
# Dense layer
num_hidden = 32
W2 = tf.Variable(tf.truncated_normal(
        [p1_size, num_hidden],
        stddev=2./math.sqrt(p1_size)))
b2 = tf.Variable(tf.constant(0.2,
        shape=[num_hidden]))
h2 = tf.nn.relu(tf.matmul(p1f,W2) + b2)
```

Of course, we'll need to initialize our weight matrix with `p1_size` the number of inputs to this layer. That's just the flattened array from the convolution and pooling output. And we'll need `num_hidden` the 32 outputs. The biased term works the same way with some small non-zero initial value. And here we happen to be using `relu` activation as well.

To finish up we define the output logistic regression as usual:

```
# Output Layer
W3 = tf.Variable(tf.truncated_normal(
    [num_hidden, 5],
    stddev=1./math.sqrt(num_hidden)))
b3 = tf.Variable(tf.constant(0.1,shape=[5]))

keep_prob = tf.placeholder("float")
h2_drop = tf.nn.dropout(h2, keep_prob)
```

Working from an old model just make sure that the final weights use `num_hidden,` 5 for the size. We have a new element here called dropout. Don't worry about it now. We'll describe exactly what it does in the next section. Just know that it helps with overfitting.

You can now initialize all your variables and implement the final call to `softmax`:

```
# Just initialize
sess.run(tf.global_variables_initializer())

# Define model
y = tf.nn.softmax(tf.matmul(h2_drop,W3) + b3)
```

Be careful that your variable names match appropriately. Okay now that setup is complete let's train it up:

```
# Climb on cross-entropy
cross_entropy = tf.reduce_mean(
        tf.nn.softmax_cross_entropy_with_logits(
        logits = y + 1e-50, labels = y_))

# How we train
train_step = tf.train.GradientDescentOptimizer(
            0.01).minimize(cross_entropy)

# Define accuracy
correct_prediction = tf.equal(tf.argmax(y,1),
                            tf.argmax(y_,1))
accuracy = tf.reduce_mean(tf.cast(
        correct_prediction, "float"))
```

We train the model virtually exactly the same way we did the previous models. The cross_entropy node measures how wrong our predictions are and GradientDescentOptimizer adjusts the weights of our matrices. We should also take care to define nodes for our accuracy so we can measure that later. Let's train the model now with about 5,000 iterations:

```
# Actually train
epochs = 5000
train_acc = np.zeros(epochs//10)
test_acc = np.zeros(epochs//10)
for i in tqdm(range(epochs), ascii=True):
    # Record summary data, and the accuracy
    if i % 10 == 0:
        # Check accuracy on train set
        A = accuracy.eval(feed_dict={x: train,
            y_: onehot_train, keep_prob: 1.0})
        train_acc[i//10] = A
        # And now the validation set
        A = accuracy.eval(feed_dict={x: test,
```

```
        y_: onehot_test, keep_prob: 1.0})
      test_acc[i//10] = A
  train_step.run(feed_dict={x: train,
      y_: onehot_train, keep_prob: 0.5})
```

This may take an hour or more. but just imagine if you had to train a different weight for every window in your convolution. With the model trained let's look at the accuracy curves.

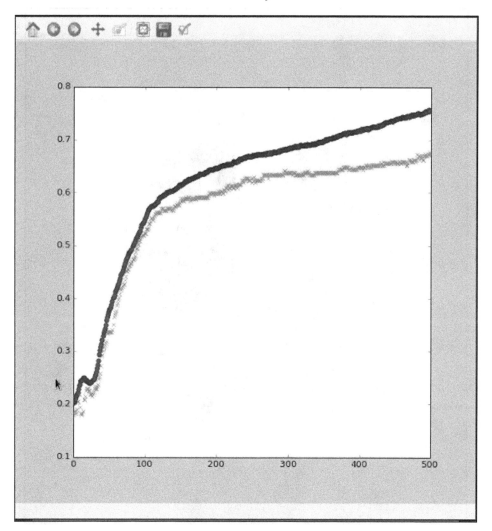

We can see that this model outperforms the old densely connected model now reaching 76 percent training accuracy and about 68 percent validation.

This is probably because the font even though it creates many different letters uses many small-scale features in the same way. Let's look at the confusion matrix too.

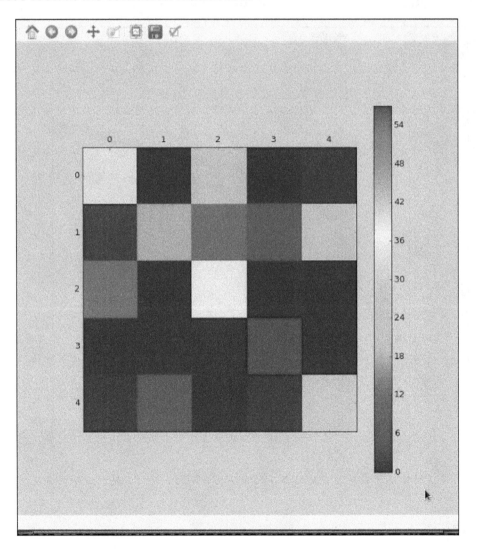

Here we see that the model is still not perfect but it's making progress. Class one is still underrepresented but it's at least partially correct unlike in some previous models where it was never correct. The other classes are mostly good. Class three is actually perfect. This isn't an easy problem so any improvement is good. We also set some code to examine the weights specifically, but we're going to save that for a later section. However feel free to play around with them here. You can save model weights and information in a checkpoint file.

```
# Save the weights
saver = tf.train.Saver()
saver.save(sess, "conv1.ckpt")


# Restore
saver.restore(sess, "conv1.ckpt")
```

This is pretty simple. You just create a `saver` object and then you save the session to a filename. Restoring is just as easy. You tell TensorFlow what session to put your saved file in and off you go. If you prefer to use NumPy to manually save your weights, the code file also provides functions for that:

```
# Or use Numpy manually
def save_all(name = 'conv1'):
    np.savez_compressed(name, W1.eval(),
            b1.eval(), W2.eval(), b2.eval(),
            W3.eval(), b3.eval())

save_all()

def load_all(name = 'conv1.npz'):
    data = np.load(name)
    sess.run(W1.assign(data['arr_0']))
    sess.run(b1.assign(data['arr_1']))
    sess.run(W2.assign(data['arr_2']))
```

```
        sess.run(b2.assign(data['arr_3']))
        sess.run(W3.assign(data['arr_4']))
        sess.run(b3.assign(data['arr_5']))

    load_all()
```

This can be more convenient because the NumPy format is very portable and reasonably lightweight. If you're exporting values to another Python script so that it doesn't need TensorFlow you might prefer NumPy. In this section we built a convolutional neural network to classify our fonts. An analogous model run on current research problems today. You are at the forefront of deep learning with TensorFlow.

Deeper CNN

In this section, we're going to add another convolutional layer to our model. Don't worry, we'll walk through the parameters to make sizing line up and we'll learn what dropout training is.

Adding a layer to another layer of CNN

As usual, when starting a new model, make a fresh IPython session and execute the code up to `num_filters1`. Great, now you're all set to start learning. Let's jump into our convolutional model.

Why don't we be ambitious and set the first convolutional layer to have 16 filters, far more than the 4 from our old model. But, we'll use a smaller window size this time. Just 3x3. Also note that we changed some variable names such as num_filters to num_filters1. This is because we're going to have another convolutional layer in just a moment and we might want a different number of filters on each. The rest of this layer is exactly as it was before, we can convolve and do 2x2 max pooling and we use the rectified linear activation unit.

Now we add another convolutional layer. Some models do several convolutions followed by a pooling layer, others do one convolution, then one pooling, then one convolution, and so on. We're doing the latter here. Suppose you want four filters and a 3x3 window. This is easy to make weights for; the only big difference from the previous layer is that we now have many input channels, see num_filters1 here:

```
# Conv layer 2
num_filters2 = 4
winx2 = 3
winy2 = 3
W2 = tf.Variable(tf.truncated_normal(
    [winx2, winy2, num_filters1, num_filters2],
    stddev=1./math.sqrt(winx2*winy2)))
b2 = tf.Variable(tf.constant(0.1,
    shape=[num_filters2]))
```

That's because we have 16 input channels coming from the previous layer. If we had used num_filters1 = 8, we'd have only 8 input channels. Think of this as a low-level feature that we're going to build on. And remember the number of channels and the input is like the number of colors, so if you want to think about it like that, that might help you.

When we do the actual second convolutional layer, make sure to pass in the output from the first pooling layer `p1`. Now this can go into a new `relu` activation function followed by another pooling layer. As usual we do 2x2 max pooling with valid padding:

```
# 3x3 convolution, pad with zeros on edges
p1w2 = tf.nn.conv2d(p1, W2,
        strides=[1, 1, 1, 1], padding='SAME')
h1 = tf.nn.relu(p1w2 + b2)
# 2x2 Max pooling, no padding on edges
p2 = tf.nn.max_pool(h1, ksize=[1, 2, 2, 1],
        strides=[1, 2, 2, 1], padding='VALID')
```

Flattening the pooling output for a convolution follows the same process as the last model too. This time, however, we work on pooling output 2 of course. Getting it's number of parameters from all its features in the window into one big vector:

```
# Need to flatten convolutional output
p2_size = np.product(
        [s.value for s in p2.get_shape()[1:]])
p2f = tf.reshape(p2, [-1, p2_size ])
```

Now we insert a densely connected layer into our neural network just like we've done in previous sections. Just make sure to update the variable names.

```
# Dense layer
num_hidden = 32
W3 = tf.Variable(tf.truncated_normal(
        [p2_size, num_hidden],
        stddev=2./math.sqrt(p2_size)))
b3 = tf.Variable(tf.constant(0.2,
        shape=[num_hidden]))
h3 = tf.nn.relu(tf.matmul(p2f,W3) + b3)
```

Now we see the same `tf.nn.dropout` that we used but didn't explain in the last model:

```
# Drop out training
keep_prob = tf.placeholder("float")
h3_drop = tf.nn.dropout(h3, keep_prob)
```

Dropout is a way to temporarily cut a neuron out of our model. We do this during training to help avoid overfitting. Each batch TensorFlow will pick different neuronal output at this connection layer to remove. This helps the model be robust in the face of small changes during training. The `keep_prob` is the probability of keeping a particular neuron output. It's common to set this to `0.5` during training.

And again, the final logistic regression layer and the training node code is all the same as earlier:

```
# Output Layer
W4 = tf.Variable(tf.truncated_normal(
        [num_hidden, 5],
        stddev=1./math.sqrt(num_hidden)))
b4 = tf.Variable(tf.constant(0.1,shape=[5]))

# Just initialize
sess.run(tf.initialize_all_variables())

# Define model
y = tf.nn.softmax(tf.matmul(h3_drop,W4) + b4)

### End model specification, begin training code


# Climb on cross-entropy
cross_entropy = tf.reduce_mean(
        tf.nn.softmax_cross_entropy_with_logits(
```

```
            y + 1e-50, y_))

# How we train
train_step = tf.train.GradientDescentOptimizer(
            0.01).minimize(cross_entropy)

# Define accuracy
correct_prediction = tf.equal(tf.argmax(y,1),
                              tf.argmax(y_,1))
accuracy = tf.reduce_mean(tf.cast(
            correct_prediction, "float"))
```

You can execute that now. Now we can train our full convolutional neural net, the apex of our modelling thus far:

```
# Actually train
epochs = 6000
train_acc = np.zeros(epochs//10)
test_acc = np.zeros(epochs//10)
for i in tqdm(range(epochs), ascii=True):
    # Record summary data, and the accuracy
    if i % 10 == 0:
        # Check accuracy on train set
        A = accuracy.eval(feed_dict={x: train,
            y_: onehot_train, keep_prob: 1.0})
        train_acc[i//10] = A
        # And now the validation set
        A = accuracy.eval(feed_dict={x: test,
            y_: onehot_test, keep_prob: 1.0})
        test_acc[i//10] = A
    train_step.run(feed_dict={x: train,\
        y_: onehot_train, keep_prob: 0.5})
```

This model can take several hours to train, so you might want to start it now before the next section.

Wrapping up deep CNN

We're going to wrap-up deep CNN by evaluating our model's accuracy. Last time, we set up the final font recognition model. Now, let's see how it does. In this section, we're going to learn how to handle dropouts during training. Then, we'll see what accuracy the model achieved. Finally, we'll visualize the weights to understand what the model learned.

Make sure you pick up in your IPython session after training in the previous model. Recall that when we trained our model, we used `dropout` to remove some outputs.

While this helps with overfitting, during testing we want to make sure to use every neuron. This both increases the accuracy and makes sure that we don't forget to evaluate part of the model. And that's why in the following code lines we have, `keep_prob` is `1.0`, to always keep all the neurons.

```
# Check accuracy on train set
    A = accuracy.eval(feed_dict={x: train,
        y_: onehot_train, keep_prob: 1.0})
    train_acc[i//10] = A
    # And now the validation set
    A = accuracy.eval(feed_dict={x: test,
        y_: onehot_test, keep_prob: 1.0})
    test_acc[i//10] = A
```

Let's see how the final model did; just take a look at the training and testing accuracy as usual:

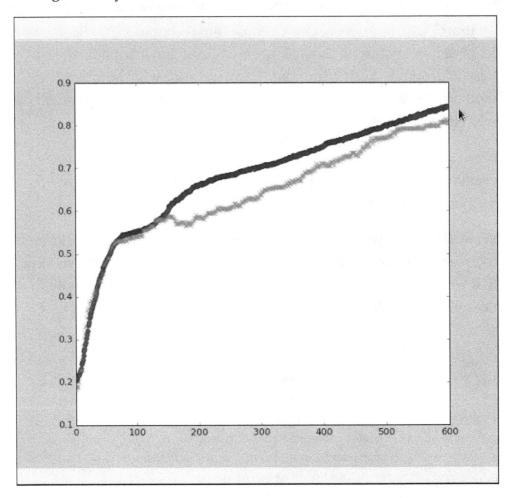

The training accuracy here topped 85 percent, and the testing accuracy isn't too far behind. Not too bad. How good a model does, depends on how noisy the input data is. If we only have a small amount of information, both in the number of examples and number of parameters or pixels, then we can't expect a model to perform perfectly.

In this case, one metric you can apply is how well a human could classify images of a single letter to each of these fonts. Some of the fonts are very distinctive, while others are similar, especially for certain letters. Because this is a novel dataset, there isn't a direct benchmark to compare against, but you can challenge yourself to beat the model presented in this course. If you do so, you might want to reduce the training time. Smaller networks with fewer parameters and simpler computations, of course, will be faster. Alternatively, if you start using a GPU or at least a multicore CPU, you can get dramatic speedups. Often 10X is better, depending on the hardware.

Part of this is parallelism, and part of it is highly-efficient low-level libraries fine-tuned for neural networks. But the easiest thing to do is start simple and work your way up to more complex models, just like you've been doing with this problem. Back to this model, let's see the confusion matrix:

```
# Look at the final testing confusion matrix
pred = np.argmax(y.eval(
        feed_dict={x: test, keep_prob: 1.0,
        y_: onehot_test}), axis = 1)
conf = np.zeros([5,5])
for p,t in zip(pred,np.argmax(onehot_test,
                                axis=1)):
    conf[t,p] += 1

plt.matshow(conf)
plt.colorbar()
```

The following is the output:

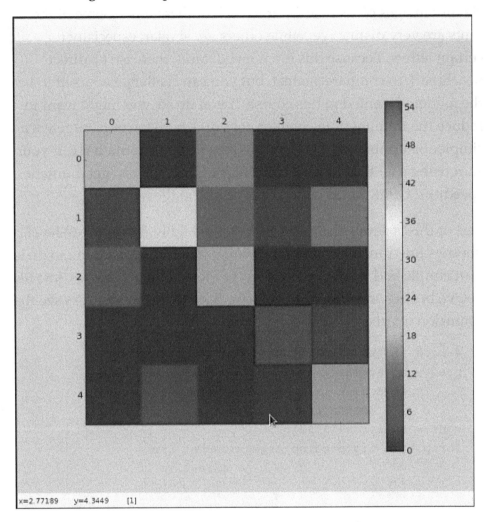

Here, we can see that the model is generally doing a good job on the various classes. Class 1 still isn't perfect, but it's much better than in the previous models. By building up smaller scale features into larger pieces, we have finally found some good indicators for the classes. Your images might not look exactly the same. It's possible to get a little unlucky with the results, depending on the random initialization of your weights.

Let's look at the weights for the 16 features of the first convolutional layer:

```
# Let's look at a subplot of some weights
f, plts = plt.subplots(4,4)
for i in range(16):
    plts[i//4,i%4].matshow(W1.eval()[:,:,0,i],
            cmap = plt.cm.gray_r)
```

Because the window size is 3x3, each one is a 3x3 matrix. Uh-huh! We can see the weights are definitely pulling out small-scale features.

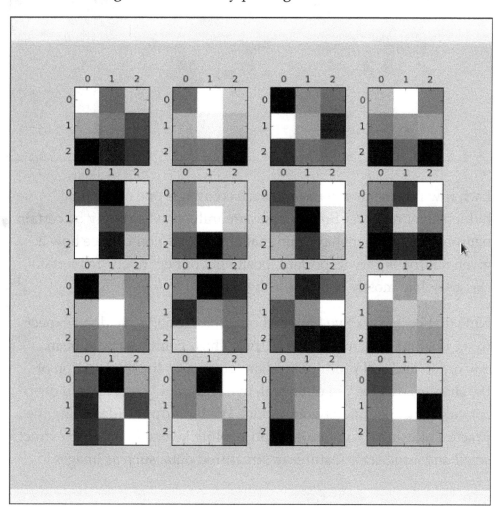

You can see certain things like edges being detected or rounded corners, different things like that. If we redo the model with a larger window, this might be even more apparent. But it's impressive how many features you can spot in just these small patches.

Let's also look at the final layer weights, just to see how the different font classes interpret the final densely connected neurons.

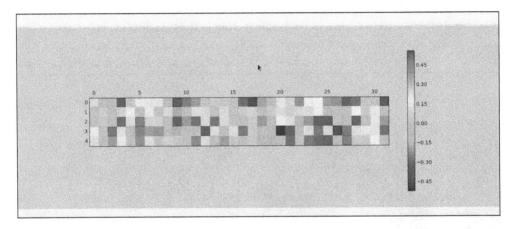

Each row represents a class, and each column is one of the final hidden layer neurons. Some classes are influenced strongly by certain neurons, while others have minimal effect. And you can see how a given neuron is very important, positively or negatively, for certain classes, while mostly neutral for the others.

Note that because we've flattened our convolutions, we don't expect to see obvious structure in the output. These columns could be in any order, and still produce the same results. In the final section of the chapter, we checked out a real, live and frankly, pretty nice deep convolutional neural network model. We built up the idea using the practice of using convolutional and pooling layers, in order to extract small and large-scale features in structured data, such as images.

For many problems, this is among the most powerful types of neural networks.

Summary

In this chapter, we walked through the convolutional layer on an example image. We tackled the practical aspects of understanding the convolutions. They can be convoluted but hopefully no longer confusing. We eventually applied this concept to a simple example in TensorFlow. We explored a common partner to convolutions, pooling layers. We explained the workings of max pooling layers, a common convolutional partner. Then, as we progressed, we put this into practice by adding a pooling layer to our example. We also practiced creating a max pooling layer in TensorFlow. We started adding convolutional neural nets to the font classification problem.

In the next chapter, we'll look at models with a time component, **Recurrent Neural Networks (RNNs)**.

4
Introducing Recurrent Neural Networks

In the previous chapter, you learned about convolutional networks. Now, it's time to move on to a new type of model and problem— **Recurrent Neural Networks (RNNs)**. In this chapter, we'll explain the workings of RNNs, and implement one in TensorFlow. Our example problem will be a simple season predictor with weather information. We will also take a look at `skflow`, a simplified interface to TensorFlow. This will let us quickly re-implement both our old image classification models and the new RNN. At the end of this chapter, you will have a good understanding of the following concepts:

- Exploring RNNs
- TensorFlow learn
- **Dense Neural Network (DNN)**

Exploring RNNs

In this section, we'll explore RNNs. Some background information will start us off, and then we will look at a motivating weather modeling problem. We'll also implement and train an RNN in TensorFlow.

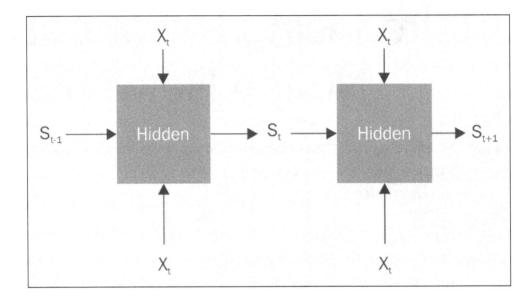

In a typical model, you have some X input features and some Y output you want to predict. We usually consider our different training samples as independent observations. So, the features from data point one shouldn't impact the prediction for data point two. But what if our data points are correlated? The most common example is that each data point, **Xt**, represents features collected at time **t**. It's natural to suppose that the features at time t and time $t+1$ will both be important to the prediction at time $t+1$. In other words, history matters.

Now, when modeling, you could just include twice as many input features, adding the previous time step to the current ones, and computing twice as many input weights. But, if you're going through all the effort of building a neural network to compute transform features, it would be nice if you could use the intermediate features from the previous time step, in the current time step network.

RNNs do exactly this. Consider your input, **Xt** as usual, but add in some state, **St-1** that comes from the previous time step, as additional features. Now you can compute weights as usual to predict **Yt**, and you produce a new internal state, **St**, to be used in the next time step. For the first time step, it's typical to use a default or zero initial state. Classic RNNs are literally this simple, but there are more advanced structures common in literature today, such as gated recurrent units and long short-term memory circuits. These are beyond the scope of this book, but work on the same principles and generally apply to the same types of problems.

Modeling the weights

You might be wondering how we'll compute weights with all these dependents on the previous time step. Computing the gradients does involve recursing back through the time computation, but fear not, TensorFlow handles the tedious stuff and let's us do the modeling:

```
# read in data
filename = 'weather.npz'
data = np.load(filename)
daily = data['daily']
weekly = data['weekly']

num_weeks = len(weekly)
dates = np.array([datetime.datetime.strptime(str(int(d)),
          '%Y%m%d') for d in weekly[:,0]])
```

To use RNNs, we need a data modeling problem with a time component.

The font classification problem isn't really appropriate here. So, let's take a look at some weather data. The `weather.npz` file is a collection of weather station data from a city in the United States over several decades. The `daily` array contains measurements from every day of the year. There are six columns to the data, starting with the date. Next, is the precipitation, measuring any rainfall in inches that day. After this, come two columns for snow — the first is measured snow currently on the ground, while the latter is snowfall on that day, again, in inches. Finally, we have some temperature information, the daily high and the daily low in degrees Fahrenheit.

The `weekly` array, which we'll use, is a weekly summary of the daily information. We'll use the middle date to indicate the week, then, we'll sum up all rainfall for the week. For snow, however, we'll average the snow on the ground, since it doesn't make sense to add snow from one cold day to the same snow sitting on the ground the next day. Snowfall though, we'll total for the week, just like rain. Finally, we'll average the high and low temperatures for the week respectively. Now that you've got a handle on the dataset, what shall we do with it? One interesting time-based modeling problem would be trying to predict the season of a particular week using it's weather information and the history of previous weeks.

In the Northern Hemisphere, in the United States, it's warmer during the months of June through August and colder during December through February, with transitions in between. Spring months tend to be rainy, and winter often includes snow. While one week can be highly variable, a history of weeks should provide some predictive power.

Understanding RNNs

First, let's read in the data from a compressed NumPy array. The `weather.npz` file happens to include the daily data as well, if you wish to explore your own model; `np.load` reads both arrays into a dictionary and will set weekly to be our data of interest; `num_weeks` is naturally how many data points we have, here, several decades worth of information:

```
num_weeks = len(weekly)
```

To format the weeks, we use a Python `datetime.datetime` object reading the storage string in year month day format:

```
dates = np.array([datetime.datetime.strptime(str(int(d)),
                '%Y%m%d') for d in weekly[:,0]])
```

We can use the date of each week to assign its season. For this model, because we're looking at weather data, we use the meteorological season rather than the common astronomical season. Thankfully, this is easy to implement with the Python function. Grab the month from the `datetime` object and we can directly compute this season. Spring, season zero, is March through May, summer is June through August, autumn is September through November, and finally, winter is December through February. The following is the simple function that just evaluates the month and implements that:

```
def assign_season(date):
    ''' Assign season based on meteorological season.
        Spring - from Mar 1 to May 31
        Summer - from Jun 1 to Aug 31
        Autumn - from Sep 1 to Nov 30
        Winter - from Dec 1 to Feb 28 (Feb 29 in a leap
year)
    '''
    month = date.month
    # spring = 0
```

```
    if 3 <= month < 6:
        season = 0
    # summer = 1
    elif 6 <= month < 9:
        season = 1
    # autumn = 2
    elif 9 <= month < 12:
        season = 2
    # winter = 3
    elif month == 12 or month < 3:
        season = 3
    return season
```

Let's note that we have four seasons and five input variables and, say, 11 values in our history state:

```
# There are 4 seasons
num_classes = 4

# and 5 variables
num_inputs = 5

# And a state of 11 numbers
state_size = 11
```

Now you're ready to compute the labels:

```
labels = np.zeros([num_weeks,num_classes])
# read and convert to one-hot
for i,d in enumerate(dates):
    labels[i,assign_season(d)] = 1
```

We do this directly in one-hot format, by making an all-zeroes array and putting a one in the position of the assign season.

Cool! You just summarized decades of time with a few commands.

As these input features measure very different things, namely rainfall, snow, and temperature, on very different scales, we should take care to put them all on the same scale. In the following code, we grab the input features, skipping the date column of course, and subtract the average to center all features at zero:

```
# extract and scale training data
train = weekly[:,1:]
train = train - np.average(train,axis=0)
train = train / train.std(axis=0)
```

Then, we scale each feature by dividing by its standard deviation. This accounts for temperatures ranging roughly 0 to 100, while rainfall only changes between about 0 and 10. Nice work on the data prep! It isn't always fun, but it's a key part of machine learning and TensorFlow.

Let's now jump into the TensorFlow model:

```
# These will be inputs
x = tf.placeholder("float", [None, num_inputs])
# TF likes a funky input to RNN
x_ = tf.reshape(x, [1, num_weeks, num_inputs])
```

We input our data as normal with a placeholder variable, but then you see this strange reshaping of the entire data set into one big tensor. Don't worry, this is because we technically have one long, unbroken sequence of observations. The y_ variable is just our output:

```
y_ = tf.placeholder("float", [None,num_classes])
```

We'll be computing a probability for every week for each season.

The cell variable is the key to the recurrent neural network:

```
cell = tf.nn.rnn_cell.BasicRNNCell(state_size)
```

This tells TensorFlow how the current time step depends on the previous. In this case, we'll use a basic RNN cell. So, we're only looking back one week at a time. Suppose that it has state size or 11 values. Feel free to experiment with more exotic cells and different state sizes.

To put that cell to use, we'll use `tf.nn.dynamic_rnn`:

```
outputs, states = tf.nn.dynamic_rnn(cell,x_,
                dtype=tf.nn.dtypes.float32, initial_state=None)
```

This intelligently handles the recursion rather than simply unrolling all the time steps into a giant computational graph. As we have thousands of observations in one sequence, this is critical to attain reasonable speed. After the cell, we specify our input `x_`, then `dtype` to use 32 bits to store decimal numbers in a float, and then the empty `initial_state`. We use the outputs from this to build a simple model. From this point on, the model is almost exactly as you would expect from any neural network:

We'll multiply the output of the RNN cells, some weights, and add a bias to get a score for each class for that week:

```
W1 = tf.Variable(tf.truncated_normal([state_size,num_
classes],
                        stddev=1./math.sqrt(num_inputs)))
b1 = tf.Variable(tf.constant(0.1,shape=[num_classes]))
# reshape the output for traditional usage
h1 = tf.reshape(outputs,[-1,state_size])
```

> Note that we do need to do this reshaping in order to get things in a proper size again, since we have one long sequence.

Our categorical `cross_entropy` loss function and train optimizer should be very familiar to you:

```
# Climb on cross-entropy
cross_entropy = tf.reduce_mean(
        tf.nn.softmax_cross_entropy_with_logits(y + 1e-50,
                                                y_))

# How we train
train_step = tf.train.GradientDescentOptimizer(0.01
                        ).minimize(cross_entropy)

# Define accuracy
correct_prediction = tf.equal(tf.argmax(y,1),
                                tf.argmax(y_,1))
accuracy=tf.reduce_mean(tf.cast(correct_prediction,
"float"))
```

Great work setting up the TensorFlow model! To train this, we'll use a familiar loop:

```
# Actually train
epochs = 100
train_acc = np.zeros(epochs//10)
for i in tqdm(range(epochs), ascii=True):
    if i % 10 == 0:
  # Record summary data, and the accuracy
        # Check accuracy on train set
        A = accuracy.eval(feed_dict={x: train, y_: labels})
        train_acc[i//10] = A
    train_step.run(feed_dict={x: train, y_: labels})
```

Since this is a fictitious problem, we'll not worry too much about how accurate the model really is. The goal here is just to see how an RNN works. You can see that it runs just like any TensorFlow model:

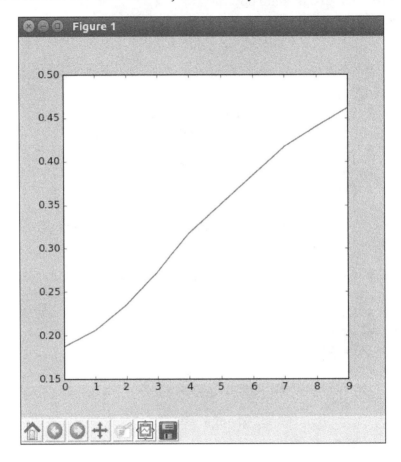

If you do look at the accuracy, you can see that it's doing pretty well; much better than the 25 percent random guessing, but still has a lot to learn.

TensorFlow learn

Just as Scikit-Learn is a convenient interface to traditional machine learning algorithms, `tf.contrib.learn` (`https://github.com/tensorflow/tensorflow/tree/master/tensorflow/contrib/learn/python/learn`), formerly known as `skflow`, it is a simplified interface to build and train DNNs. Now it comes free with every installation of TensorFlow!

Even if you're not a fan of the syntax, it's worth looking at TensorFlow Learn as the high-level API to TensorFlow. This is because it's currently the only officially supported one. But, you should know that there are many alternative high-level APIs that may have more intuitive interfaces. If interested, refer to Keras (`https://keras.io/`), `tf.slim` (included with TF), to learn more about TensorFlow-Slim refer to `https://github.com/tensorflow/tensorflow/tree/master/tensorflow/contrib/slim` or TFLearn (`http://tflearn.org/`).

Setup

To get started with TensorFlow Learn, you only need to import it. We'll also import the `estimators` function, which will help us craft general models:

```
# TF made EZ
import tensorflow.contrib.learn as learn
from tensorflow.contrib.learn.python.learn.estimators
import estimator
```

We also want to import a few libraries for basic manipulation — grab NumPy, math, and Matplotlib (optional). Of note here is `sklearn`, a general-purpose machine learning library that tries to simplify model creation, training, and usage. We'll be mainly using it for convenient metrics, but you'll find that it has a similar primary interface to Learn:

```
# Some basics
import numpy as np
import math
import matplotlib.pyplot as plt
plt.ion()

# Learn more sklearn
# scikit-learn.org
import sklearn
from sklearn import metrics
```

Next, we'll read in some data for processing. Since you're familiar with the font classification problem, let's stick with modeling that. For reproducibility, you can seed NumPy with your favorite number:

```
# Seed the data
np.random.seed(42)

# Load data
data = np.load('data_with_labels.npz')
train = data['arr_0']/255.
labels = data['arr_1']
```

For this exercise, split up your data into a training and validation set; `np.random.permutation` is useful for generating a random order for your input data, so let's use that much as we did in earlier modules:

```
# Split data into training and validation
indices = np.random.permutation(train.shape[0])
valid_cnt = int(train.shape[0] * 0.1)
test_idx, training_idx = indices[:valid_cnt],\
                         indices[valid_cnt:]
test, train = train[test_idx,:],\
                  train[training_idx,:]
test_labels, train_labels = labels[test_idx],\
                        labels[training_idx]
```

Here, `tf.contrib.learn` can be fickle about what data types it accepts. To play nicely, we need to recast our data. The image inputs will be `np.float32` instead of the default 64 bits. Also, our labels will be `np.int32` instead of `np.uint8`, even though this just takes up more memory:

```
train = np.array(train,dtype=np.float32)
test = np.array(test,dtype=np.float32)
train_labels = np.array(train_labels,dtype=np.int32)
test_labels = np.array(test_labels,dtype=np.int32)
```

Logistic regression

Let's do a simple logistic regression example. This will be very quick and show how `learn` makes straightforward models incredibly simple. First, we must create a listing of variables that our model expects as input. You might hope that this could be set with a simple argument, but it's actually this unintuitive `learn.infer_real_valued_columns_from_input` function. Basically, if you give your input data to this function, it will infer how many feature columns you have and what shape it should be in. In our linear model, we want to flatten our image to be one-dimensional, so we reshape it when inferring the features:

```
# Convert features to learn style
feature_columns = learn.infer_real_valued_columns_from_
input(train.reshape([-1,36*36]))
```

Now make a new variable called, `classifier`, and assign to it this `estimator.SKCompat` construction. This is a Scikit-Learn compatibility layer, allowing you to use some of the Scikit-Learn modules with your TensorFlow model.

Anyway, that's just dressing, what really creates the model is `learn.LinearClassifier`. This sets up the model, but does no training. So, it only requires a couple of arguments. The first is that funky `feature_columns` object, just letting your model know what to expect for input. The second, and final required argument is its converse, how many output values the model should have? We have five fonts, so set `n_classes = 5`. That's the entire model specification!

```
# Logistic Regression
classifier = estimator.SKCompat(learn.LinearClassifier(
        feature_columns = feature_columns,
        n_classes=5))
```

To do the training, it takes just a single line. Call `classifier.fit` with your input data (reshaped, of course), output labels (note that these don't have to be one-hot format), and a few more parameters. The `steps` argument determines how many batches the model will look at, that is, how many steps to take of the optimization algorithm. The `batch_size` argument is, as usual, the number of data points to use within an optimization step. So, you can compute the number of epochs as the number of steps times the size of batches divided by the number of data points in your training set. This may seem a little counterintuitive, but at least it's a quick specification, and you could easily write a helper function to convert between steps and epochs:

```
# One line training
# steps is number of total batches
# steps*batch_size/len(train) = num_epochs
classifier.fit(train.reshape([-1,36*36]),
               train_labels,
               steps=1024,
               batch_size=32)
```

To evaluate our model, we'll use `metrics` of `sklearn` as usual. But the output of a basic learn model prediction is now a dictionary, within which are precomputed class labels, as well as the probabilities and logits. To extract the class labels, use the key, `classes`:

```
# sklearn compatible accuracy
test_probs = classifier.predict(test.reshape([-1,36*36]))
sklearn.metrics.accuracy_score(test_labels,
        test_probs['classes'])
```

DNNs

While there are better ways to implement purely linear models, simplifying DNNs with a varying number of layers is where TensorFlow and `learn` really shine.

We'll use the same input features, but now we'll build a DNN with two hidden layers, first with `10` neurons and then `5`. Creating this model will only take one line of Python code; it could not be easier.

The specification is similar to our linear model. We still need `SKCompat`, but now it's `learn.DNNClassifier`. For arguments, there's one additional requirement: the number of neurons on each hidden layer, passed as a list. This one simple argument, which really captures the essence of a DNN model, puts the power of deep learning at your fingertips.

There are some optional arguments to this as well, but we'll only mention `optimizer`. This allows you to choose between different common optimizer routines, such as **Stochastic Gradient Descent (SGD)** or Adam. Very convenient!

```python
# Dense neural net
classifier = estimator.SKCompat(learn.DNNClassifier(
        feature_columns = feature_columns,
        hidden_units=[10,5],
        n_classes=5,
        optimizer='Adam'))
```

The training and evaluation occur exactly as they do with the linear model. Just for demonstration, we can also look at the confusion matrix created by this model. Note that we haven't trained much, so this model may not compete with our earlier creations using pure TensorFlow:

```
# Same training call
classifier.fit(train.reshape([-1,36*36]),
               train_labels,
               steps=1024,
               batch_size=32)

# simple accuracy
test_probs = classifier.predict(test.reshape([-1,36*36]))
sklearn.metrics.accuracy_score(test_labels,
        test_probs['classes'])

# confusion is easy
train_probs = classifier.predict(train.reshape([-1,36*36]))
conf = metrics.confusion_matrix(train_labels,
        train_probs['classes'])
print(conf)
```

Convolutional Neural Networks (CNNs) in Learn

CNNs power some of the most successful machine learning models out there, so we'd hope that learn supports them. In fact, the library supports using arbitrary TensorFlow code! You'll find that this is a blessing and a curse. Having arbitrary code available means you can use learn to do almost anything you can do with pure TensorFlow, giving maximum flexibility. But the general interface tends to make the code more difficult to read and write.

If you find yourself fighting with the interface to make some moderately complex model work in `learn`, it may be time to use pure TensorFlow or switch to another API.

To demonstrate this generality, we'll build a simple CNN to attack our font classification problem. It will have one convolutional layer with four filters, followed by a flattening to a hidden dense layer with five neurons, and finally ending with the densely connected output logistic regression.

To get started, let's do a couple more imports. We want access to generic TensorFlow, but we also need the `layers` module to call TensorFlow `layers` in a way that `learn` expects:

```
# Access general TF functions
import tensorflow as tf
import tensorflow.contrib.layers as layers
```

The generic interface forces us to write a function which creates the operations for our model. You may find this tedious, but that's the price of flexibility.

Start a new function called `conv_learn` with three arguments. `x` will be the input data, `y` will be the output labels (not yet one-hot encoded), and `mode` determines whether you are training or predicting. Note that you'll never directly interact with this function; you merely pass it to a constructor that expects these arguments. So, if you wanted to vary the number or type of layers, you would need to write a new model function (or another function that would generate such a model function):

```
def conv_learn(X, y, mode):
```

As this is a convolutional model, we need to make sure our data is formatted correctly. In particular, this means reshaping the input to have not only the correct two-dimensional shape (36x36), but also 1 color channel (the last dimension). This is part of a TensorFlow computation graph, so we use `tf.reshape`, not `np.reshape`. Likewise, because this is a generic graph, we want our outputs to be one-hot encoded, and `tf.one_hot` provides that functionality. Note that we have to describe how many classes there are (5), what a set value should be (1), and what an unset value should be (0):

```
# Ensure our images are 2d
X = tf.reshape(X, [-1, 36, 36, 1])
# We'll need these in one-hot format
y = tf.one_hot(tf.cast(y, tf.int32), 5, 1, 0)
```

Now the real fun begins. To specify the convolutional layer, let's initialize a new scope, `conv_layer`. This will just make sure we don't clobber any variables. `layers.convolutional` provides the basic machinery. It accepts our input (a TensorFlow tensor), a number of outputs (really the number of kernels or filters), and the size of the kernel, here, a 5x5 window. For an activation function, let's use Rectified Linear, which we can call from the main TensorFlow module. This gives us our basic convolutional output, `h1`.

Max pooling actually occurs exactly as it does in regular TensorFlow, neither easier nor harder. The function, tf.nn.max_pool with the usual kernel size and strides works as expected. Save this into p1:

```
# conv layer will compute 4 kernels for each 5x5 patch
with tf.variable_scope('conv_layer'):
    # 5x5 convolution, pad with zeros on edges
    h1 = layers.convolution2d(X, num_outputs=4,
            kernel_size=[5, 5],
            activation_fn=tf.nn.relu)
    # 2x2 Max pooling, no padding on edges
    p1 = tf.nn.max_pool(h1, ksize=[1, 2, 2, 1],
            strides=[1, 2, 2, 1], padding='VALID')
```

Now, to flatten the tensor at this point, we need to compute the number of elements in our would-be one-dimensional tensor. One way to do this is by multiplying all the dimension values (except the batch_size, which occupies the first position) together. This particular operation can occur outside the computation graph, so we use np.product. Once supplied with the total size, we can pass it to tf.reshape to reslice the intermediate tensor in the graph:

```
# Need to flatten conv output for use in dense layer
p1_size = np.product(
            [s.value for s in p1.get_shape()[1:]])
p1f = tf.reshape(p1, [-1, p1_size ])
```

Now it's time for the densely connected layer. The layers module makes an appearance again, this time with the fully_connected function (another name for a dense layer). This takes the previous layer, the number of neurons, and the activation function, again supplied by general TensorFlow.

For demonstration purposes, let's add a dropout here as well; `layers.dropout` provides the interface. As expected, it needs the previous layer as well as a probability of keeping a given node output. But it also needs this `mode` argument that we passed into the original `conv_learn` function. All this complex interface is saying is to only drop nodes during training. If you can handle that, we're almost through the model!

```
# densely connected layer with 32 neurons and dropout

h_fc1 = layers.fully_connected(p1f,

              5,

              activation_fn=tf.nn.relu)

drop = layers.dropout(h_fc1, keep_prob=0.5,

    is_training=mode == tf.contrib.learn.ModeKeys.TRAIN)
```

Now for some bad news. We need to write out the final linear model, loss function, and optimization parameters manually. This is something that can change from version to version, as it used to be easier on the user for some circumstances, but more difficult to maintain the backend. But let's persevere; it's really not too arduous.

Another `layers.fully_connected` layer creates the final logistic regression. Note that our activation here should be `None`, as it is purely linear. What handles the *logistic* side of the equation is the loss function. Thankfully, TensorFlow supplies a `softmax_cross_entropy` function, so we don't need to write this out manually. Given inputs, outputs, and a loss function, we can apply an optimization routine. Again, `layers.optimize_loss` minimizes the pain, as well as the function in question. Pass it your loss node, optimizer (as a string), and a learning rate. Further, give it this `get_global_step()` parameter to ensure the optimizer handles decay properly.

Finally, our function needs to return a few things. One, it should report the predicted classes. Next, it must supply the loss node output itself. And, finally, the training node must be available to external routines to actually execute everything:

```
logits = layers.fully_connected(drop, 5,
                                    activation_fn=None)
loss = tf.losses.softmax_cross_entropy(y, logits)
# Setup the training function manually
train_op = layers.optimize_loss(
    loss,
    tf.contrib.framework.get_global_step(),
    optimizer='Adam',
    learning_rate=0.01)
return tf.argmax(logits, 1), loss, train_op
```

While specifying the model may be cumbersome, using it is just as easy as before. Now, use `learn.Estimator`, the most generic routine, and pass in your model function for `model_fn`. And don't forget the `SKCompat`!

Training works exactly as before, just note that we don't need to reshape the inputs here, since that's handled inside the function.

To predict with the model, you can simply call `classifier.predict`, but note that you get your first argument returned by the function as output. We opted to return the class, but it would also be reasonable to return the probabilities from the `softmax` function as well. That's all regarding the basics of the `tf.contrib.learn` models!

```
# Use generic estimator with our function
classifier = estimator.SKCompat(
        learn.Estimator(
        model_fn=conv_learn))

classifier.fit(train,train_labels,
            steps=1024,
```

```
            batch_size=32)
```

```
# simple accuracy
metrics.accuracy_score(test_labels,classifier.
predict(test))
```

Extracting weights

While training and prediction are the core uses of models, it's important to be able to study the inside of models as well. Unfortunately, this API makes it difficult to extract parameter weights. Thankfully, this section provides some simple examples of a weakly documented feature to get the weights out of the `tf.contrib.learn` models.

To pull out the weights of a model, we really need to get the value from certain points in the underlying TensorFlow computation graph. TensorFlow provides many ways to do this, but the first problem is just figuring out what your variable of interest is called.

A list of variable names in your `learn` graph is available, but it's buried under the hidden attribute, `_estimator`. Calling `classifier._estimator.get_variable_names()` returns a list of strings of your various names. Many of these will be uninteresting, such as the `OptimizeLoss` entries. In our case, we're looking for the `conv_layer` and `fully_connected` elements:

```
# See layer names
print(classifier._estimator.get_variable_names())
['OptimizeLoss/beta1_power',
 'OptimizeLoss/beta2_power',
 'OptimizeLoss/conv_layer/Conv/biases/Adam',
 'OptimizeLoss/conv_layer/Conv/biases/Adam_1',
 'OptimizeLoss/conv_layer/Conv/weights/Adam',
 'OptimizeLoss/conv_layer/Conv/weights/Adam_1',
 'OptimizeLoss/fully_connected/biases/Adam',
```

```
'OptimizeLoss/fully_connected/biases/Adam_1',
'OptimizeLoss/fully_connected/weights/Adam',
'OptimizeLoss/fully_connected/weights/Adam_1',
'OptimizeLoss/fully_connected_1/biases/Adam',
'OptimizeLoss/fully_connected_1/biases/Adam_1',
'OptimizeLoss/fully_connected_1/weights/Adam',
'OptimizeLoss/fully_connected_1/weights/Adam_1',
'OptimizeLoss/learning_rate',
'conv_layer/Conv/biases',
'conv_layer/Conv/weights',
'fully_connected/biases',
'fully_connected/weights',
'fully_connected_1/biases',
'fully_connected_1/weights',
'global_step']
```

Figuring out which entry is the layer you're looking for can be a challenge. Here, `conv_layer` is obviously from our convolutional layer. However, you see two `fully_connected` elements, one is our dense layer at flattening, and one is the output weights. It turns out that they are named in the order specified. We created the dense hidden layer first, so it gets the basic `fully_connected` name, while the output layer came last, so it has a `_1` tacked onto it. If you're unsure, you can always look at the shapes of the weight arrays, depending on the shape of your model.

To actually get at the weights, it's another arcane call. This time, `classifier._estimator.get_variable_value`, supplied with the variable name string, produces a NumPy array with the relevant weights. Try it out for the convolutional weights and biases, as well as the dense layers:

```
# Convolutional Layer Weights
print(classifier._estimator.get_variable_value(
        'conv_layer/Conv/weights'))
print(classifier._estimator.get_variable_value(
```

```
        'conv_layer/Conv/biases'))

    # Dense Layer
    print(classifier._estimator.get_variable_value(
          'fully_connected/weights'))

    # Logistic weights
    print(classifier._estimator.get_variable_value(
          'fully_connected_1/weights'))
```

Now, armed with the esoteric knowledge of how to peer inside `tf.contrib.learn` neural networks, you're more than capable with this high-level API. While it is convenient in many situations, it can be cumbersome in others. Never be afraid to pause and consider switching to another library; use the right machine learning tool for the right machine learning job.

Summary

You learned a lot in this chapter, going from simply understanding RNNs to implementing them in a new TensorFlow model. We also looked at a simple interface to TensorFlow called TensorFlow Learn. We also walked through DNNs, and understood CNNs and extracting weights in detail.

In the next chapter, we will wrap up our look at TensorFlow, looking at how far we've come and where you can go from here.

5
Wrapping Up

In the previous chapter, we learned about another interface to TensorFlow and RNN models. This chapter will wrap up our look at TensorFlow, looking at how far we've come and where you can go from here. First, we'll review our progress on the font classification problem, then we'll briefly look at TensorFlow beyond deep learning and see where it will go in the future. At the end of the chapter, you will be familiar with the following concepts:

- Research evaluation
- A quick review of all the models
- The future of TensorFlow
- Some more TensorFlow projects

Let's now begin by looking at research evaluation in detail.

Research evaluation

In this section, we'll compare our models in the font classification problem. First, we should remind ourselves what the data looks like. Then, we'll inspect the simple logistic dense neural network and convolutional neural network models. You've come a long way in modeling with TensorFlow.

Before we move on from deep learning, however, let's look back and see how models compare on the font classification problem. First, let's look at the data again, so we don't lose sight of the problem. In fact, let's look at one image that includes all the letters and digits from every font, just to see what shapes we have:

```
# One look at a letter/digit from each font
# Best to reshape as one large array, then plot
all_letters = np.zeros([5*36,62*36])
for font in range(5):
    for letter in range(62):
        all_letters[font*36:(font+1)*36,
                letter*36:(letter+1)*36] = \
                train[9*(font*62 + letter)]
```

This would be a lot of subplots for Matplotlib to handle. So, we'll make a new array, 5 images tall, 5 fonts times 36 pixels, and 62 images wide, 62 letters or digits times 36 pixels. After allocating a zero array, we can stack the training images into it. Fonts and letters act as indices and we set 36x36 values at a time in the big array. Note that we have 9 in the `train` array here, because we're only taking one type of jitter each letter.

Let's take a look with a quick call to `pcolormesh`:

```
plt.pcolormesh(all_letters,
        cmap=plt.cm.gray)
```

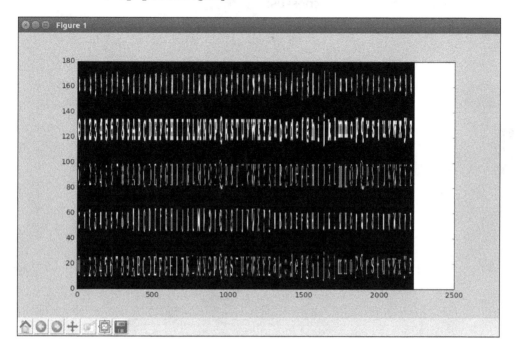

As you can see, we have the entire alphabet, upper and lowercase, as well as digits 0 to 9. Some of the fonts look like others, while font `0` is kind of in its own world, to human eyes anyway. Each font has interesting stylistic properties that we hope our model picks up on.

A quick review of all the models

Let's recap each of the models we built, to model these fonts and some of their strengths and weaknesses:

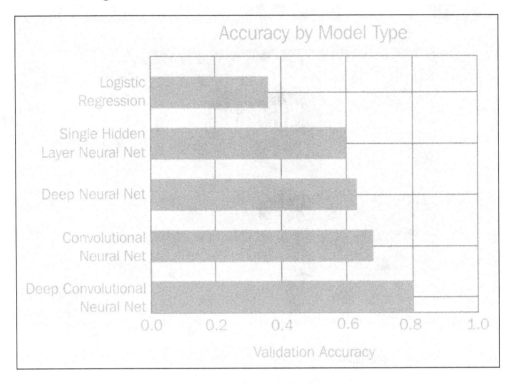

At a glance, recall that we slowly built up more complicated models and took into account the structure of the data to improve our accuracy.

The logistic regression model

First, we started with a simple logistic regression model:

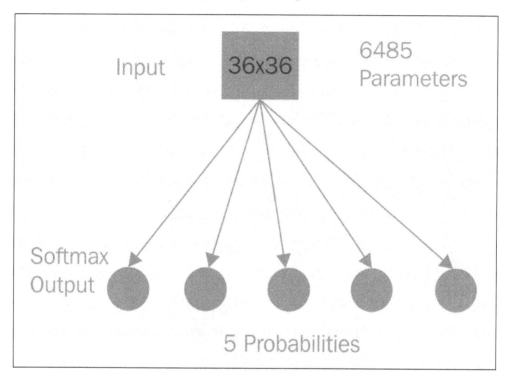

This has 36x36 pixels plus 1 bias times 5 classes total weights, or 6,485 parameters that we need to train. After 1,000 training epochs, this model achieved about 40 percent validation accuracy. Your results may vary. This is relatively poor, but the model has some advantages.

Let's glance back at the code:

```
# These will be inputs
## Input pixels, flattened
x = tf.placeholder("float", [None, 1296])
## Known labels
y_ = tf.placeholder("float", [None,5])

# Variables
W = tf.Variable(tf.zeros([1296,5]))
b = tf.Variable(tf.zeros([5]))

# Just initialize
sess.run(tf.initialize_all_variables())

# Define model
y = tf.nn.softmax(tf.matmul(x,W) + b)
```

The simplicity of logistic regression means we can directly see and compute how each pixel affects the class probabilities. This simplicity also makes the model relatively quick to converge in training, and of course, quick to program, as it takes only a few lines of TensorFlow code.

The single hidden layer neural network model

Our next model was a single hidden layer densely connected neural network with a final Softmax activation layer, equivalent to logistic regression:

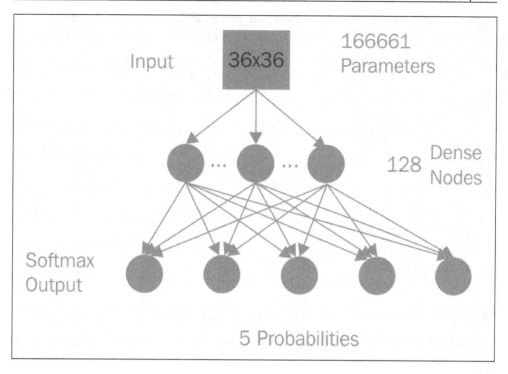

This model has 36x36 pixels plus 1 bias times 128 nodes plus 128 hidden nodes plus 1 bias times 5 classes total weights, or 166,661 parameters. The hidden layer uses a `sigmoid` activation function to achieve nonlinearity. After 5,000 epochs, this tangle of parameters reached about 60 percent validation accuracy, a considerable improvement. The cost for this improvement, however, was a huge increase in the number of parameters in computational complexity, which you can get a sense of just from the code:

```
# These will be inputs
## Input pixels, flattened
x = tf.placeholder("float", [None, 1296])
## Known labels
y_ = tf.placeholder("float", [None,5])

# Hidden layer
num_hidden = 128
```

```
W1 = tf.Variable(tf.truncated_normal([1296, num_hidden],
                                 stddev=1./math.sqrt(1296)))
b1 = tf.Variable(tf.constant(0.1,shape=[num_hidden]))
h1 = tf.sigmoid(tf.matmul(x,W1) + b1)

# Output Layer
W2 = tf.Variable(tf.truncated_normal([num_hidden, 5],
                                 stddev=1./math.sqrt(5)))
b2 = tf.Variable(tf.constant(0.1,shape=[5]))

# Just initialize
sess.run(tf.initialize_all_variables())

# Define model
y = tf.nn.softmax(tf.matmul(h1,W2) + b2)
```

We can no longer have a simple function of individual pixels to class probabilities. But this required only a few more lines of coding and does perform better.

Deep neural network

The deep neural network took this one step further, consisting of 128 nodes on the first layer, feeding into 32 nodes on a subsequent layer before feeding into Softmax for a total of 170,309 parameters; not that many more really:

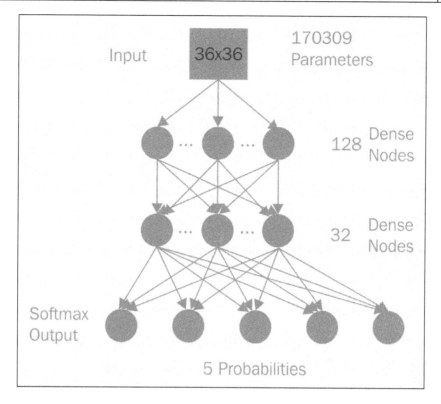

After 25,000 epochs, we achieved a marginal improvement of 63 percent validation accuracy:

```
# These will be inputs
## Input pixels, flattened
x = tf.placeholder("float", [None, 1296])
## Known labels
y_ = tf.placeholder("float", [None,5])

# Hidden layer 1
num_hidden1 = 128
W1 = tf.Variable(tf.truncated_normal([1296,num_hidden1],
                            stddev=1./math.sqrt(1296)))
b1 = tf.Variable(tf.constant(0.1,shape=[num_hidden1]))
h1 = tf.sigmoid(tf.matmul(x,W1) + b1)

# Hidden Layer 2
```

```
num_hidden2 = 32
W2 = tf.Variable(tf.truncated_normal([num_hidden1,
            num_hidden2],stddev=2./math.sqrt(num_hidden1)))
b2 = tf.Variable(tf.constant(0.2,shape=[num_hidden2]))
h2 = tf.sigmoid(tf.matmul(h1,W2) + b2)

# Output Layer
W3 = tf.Variable(tf.truncated_normal([num_hidden2, 5],
                        stddev=1./math.sqrt(5)))
b3 = tf.Variable(tf.constant(0.1,shape=[5]))

# Just initialize
sess.run(tf.initialize_all_variables())

# Define model
y = tf.nn.softmax(tf.matmul(h2,W3) + b3)
```

A deeper still model might have done better, but this demonstrated some of the strength of deep learning, handling considerable nonlinearity, and this again took marginal extra programming effort.

Convolutional neural network

The densely connected neural networks worked reasonably well, but fonts are defined by their style, not specific pixels:

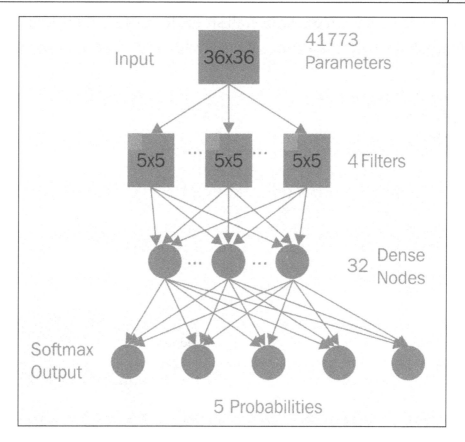

Recurring local features should be big clues to your model. We captured some of these local features with convolutional neural networks. We started with one convolutional layer, a 5x5 window computing four features with four extra biased terms extracted interesting local parameters, using a rectified linear unit. We followed this with a 2x2 max pooling layer applied to each feature, reducing the number of intermediate values to 18x18x4 plus 1 bias. Flattening this out to 1,297 numbers and putting into 32 nodes of a dense neural network followed by Softmax activations finish the model with a total of 41,773 parameters.

That's a nice cutdown on the overall size of the model, although the implementation and code takes more effort than before:

```
# Conv layer 1
num_filters = 4
winx = 5
winy = 5
W1 = tf.Variable(tf.truncated_normal(
    [winx, winy, 1 , num_filters],
    stddev=1./math.sqrt(winx*winy)))
b1 = tf.Variable(tf.constant(0.1,
                shape=[num_filters]))
# 5x5 convolution, pad with zeros on edges
xw = tf.nn.conv2d(x_im, W1,
                strides=[1, 1, 1, 1],
                padding='SAME')
h1 = tf.nn.relu(xw + b1)
# 2x2 Max pooling, no padding on edges
p1 = tf.nn.max_pool(h1, ksize=[1, 2, 2, 1],
        strides=[1, 2, 2, 1], padding='VALID')

# Need to flatten convolutional output for use in dense
layer
p1_size = np.product(
            [s.value for s in p1.get_shape()[1:]])
p1f = tf.reshape(p1, [-1, p1_size ])

# Dense layer
num_hidden = 32
W2 = tf.Variable(tf.truncated_normal(
    [p1_size, num_hidden],
    stddev=2./math.sqrt(p1_size)))
b2 = tf.Variable(tf.constant(0.2,
    shape=[num_hidden]))
h2 = tf.nn.relu(tf.matmul(p1f,W2) + b2)

# Output Layer
W3 = tf.Variable(tf.truncated_normal(
```

```
    [num_hidden, 5],
    stddev=1./math.sqrt(num_hidden)))
b3 = tf.Variable(tf.constant(0.1,shape=[5]))

keep_prob = tf.placeholder("float")
h2_drop = tf.nn.dropout(h2, keep_prob)
```

After training for just 5000 epochs, we cleared 68 percent accuracy. We did have to code up the convolution, but this wasn't so challenging. By applying a little knowledge to the structure of the problem, we simultaneously reduced the model size, yet increased the accuracy. Nice job on that one!

Deep convolutional neural network

Combining the deep and convolutional approach, we finally created a model with several convolutional layers:

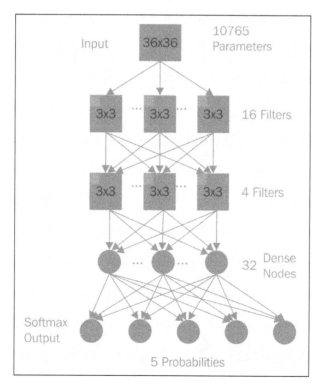

Though we used a smaller 3x3 window, we computed 16 filters on the first convolutional layer. After a 2x2 max pooling, we did it again with another 3x3 window and 4 filters on the pooled values. Another pooling layer again fed into 32 densely connected neurons and Softmax output. Because we have more convolution in pooling before feeding into a dense neural network, we actually have fewer (10,765 to be exact) parameters in this model, almost as few as the logistic regression model. Yet, with 6,000 epochs, the model topped 80 percent validation accuracy, a testament to your new deep learning and TensorFlow skills.

```
# Conv layer 1
num_filters1 = 16
winx1 = 3
winy1 = 3
W1 = tf.Variable(tf.truncated_normal(
    [winx1, winy1, 1 , num_filters1],
    stddev=1./math.sqrt(winx1*winy1)))
b1 = tf.Variable(tf.constant(0.1,
              shape=[num_filters1]))
# 5x5 convolution, pad with zeros on edges
xw = tf.nn.conv2d(x_im, W1,
                strides=[1, 1, 1, 1],
                padding='SAME')
h1 = tf.nn.relu(xw + b1)
# 2x2 Max pooling, no padding on edges
p1 = tf.nn.max_pool(h1, ksize=[1, 2, 2, 1],
        strides=[1, 2, 2, 1], padding='VALID')

# Conv layer 2
num_filters2 = 4
winx2 = 3
winy2 = 3
W2 = tf.Variable(tf.truncated_normal(
    [winx2, winy2, num_filters1, num_filters2],
    stddev=1./math.sqrt(winx2*winy2)))
```

```
b2 = tf.Variable(tf.constant(0.1,
    shape=[num_filters2]))
# 3x3 convolution, pad with zeros on edges
p1w2 = tf.nn.conv2d(p1, W2,
    strides=[1, 1, 1, 1], padding='SAME')
h1 = tf.nn.relu(p1w2 + b2)
# 2x2 Max pooling, no padding on edges
p2 = tf.nn.max_pool(h1, ksize=[1, 2, 2, 1],
    strides=[1, 2, 2, 1], padding='VALID')
```

The future of TensorFlow

In this section, we will observe how TensorFlow is changing, who is starting to use TensorFlow, and how you can make an impact contributing to it.

Since it was released in late 2015, TensorFlow has already seen several more releases:

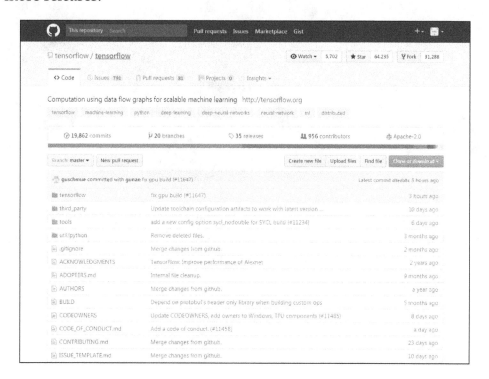

TensorFlow is constantly being updated. Although it isn't an official Google product, it is also open source and hosted on GitHub. At the time of writing, TensorFlow is at release 1.2. The most recent release added distributed computing capabilities. These are beyond the scope of this book, but generally speaking, they allow computation across multiple GPUs on multiple machines for maximum parallelization. Under heavy development, more features are always just around the corner. TensorFlow is becoming more popular every day.

Several software companies have released machine learning frameworks recently, but TensorFlow stands out in adoption. Internally, Google is practicing what they preach. Their acclaimed DeepMind team has switched to using TensorFlow.

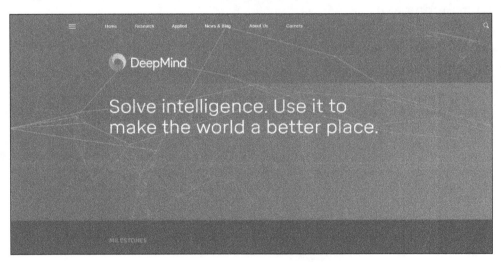

Further, many universities with machine learning or data science programs use TensorFlow, both for coursework and research projects. Of course, you've already used TensorFlow on a research project, so you are ahead of the game.

Some more TensorFlow projects

Finally, other companies, large and small, are picking up TensorFlow. Now that you are a TensorFlow practitioner, the only limits are your available problems and your computing resources. Here's a couple of ideas about what you could tackle next with TensorFlow:

- Leaf classification from images:

  Plant leaves, like fonts, have similar styles within a species. Can you adapt the models you built in this course to identify a species using just an image?

- Road sign identification with dashcam video:

  Suppose you got a lot of dashcam footage from a long road trip. Road signs on the highway can give you a lot of information, such as where you are and how fast you should be going. Can you build a series of TensorFlow models to find, say, the speed limit in the footage?

- Transportation research predicting travel times:

  Also, commuting takes too long, no matter how close you live to work. Given current conditions such as traffic and weather, you should be able to build a regression-based model to predict your travel time.

- Matching algorithm, as for finding a compatible date:

  Finally, one start-up is exploring using TensorFlow for a matching algorithm. Don't be surprised if, in the future, an algorithm gets you a date.

There are too many neat TensorFlow-based projects to list them all. But, chances are, you'll find something related to your interests, and if not, that's the perfect place to contribute. There are many machine learning libraries, but TensorFlow is here to stay.

Though this book has focused on deep learning, TensorFlow is a general graph computational library.

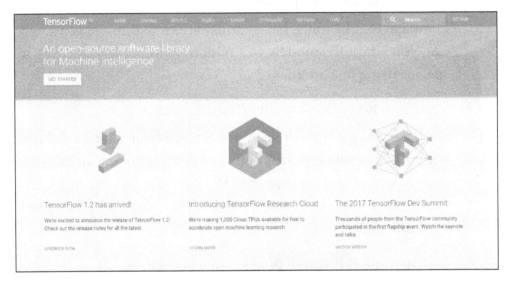

Deep neural networks are really a sliver of data modeling that TensorFlow happens to handle very well. But, as you saw in the *Simple Computations* section of *Chapter 1, Getting Started*, on simple computations, any operation you can specify as a graph, you can do in TensorFlow. One practical example was an implementation of k-means clustering in TensorFlow.

More generally, operations that vectorize well and require some kind of training may benefit from TensorFlow usage. All this is to say that you are the future of TensorFlow!

TensorFlow is open source and changing all the time. So, you can contribute new features easily on GitHub. These could be highly complex new model types or simple documentation updates.

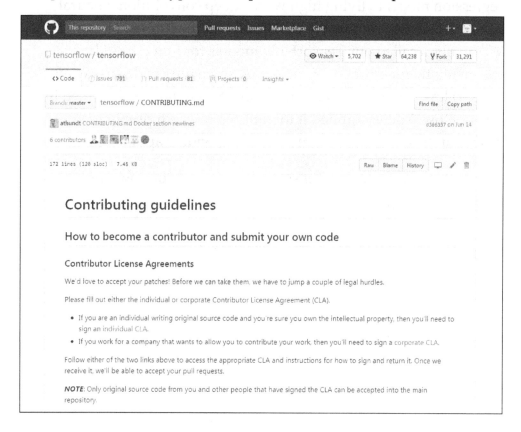

All changes can improve the library. The rising popularity of TensorFlow means that you are one of the earliest professionals to master it. You've got an edge in your machine learning career or research. And because it's more than deep learning, whatever field you're in, TensorFlow is probably applicable to some aspect of it.

Summary

In this chapter, we reviewed how we climbed from a humble logistic regression model to flying high with a deep convolutional neural network to classify fonts. We also discussed the future of TensorFlow. We finally recalled our TensorFlow models for font classification, reviewing their accuracy. We also took some time to discuss where TensorFlow is headed. Congratulations! You're now well-versed in TensorFlow. You've applied it to multiple research problems and models in this series, and learned how it's widely applicable.

The next step is to deploy TensorFlow in one of your own projects. Happy modeling!

Index

K

Keras
URL 117

L

log function 35, 36
logistic regression
about 17, 22, 120
implementing 23
logistic regression model
about 137, 138
weights, viewing of 48, 49
logistic regression model building
about 17
font classification dataset 18-21
logistic regression training
about 26
loss function, developing 26
model accuracy, evaluating 28-32
model, training 27

M

main page, TensorFlow 2
models
about 136
convolutional neural network 142-145
deep convolutional neural
network 145, 146
deep neural network 140-142
logistic regression model 137, 138
single hidden layer neural network
model 138, 140
multiple hidden layer model
about 50
exploring 51-55
results 56
multiple hidden layers graph 56-62

N

neuron 36

P

pip
TensorFlow, installing via 4, 5
pooling layer application 83, 86
pooling layers
about 78
max pooling layers 78-82

R

Recurrent Neural Networks (RNNs)
about 107-116
using 110
weights, modeling 109
research evaluation 134

S

same padding 66
scalars
defining 11, 12
sigmoid function 36, 37
single hidden layer model
about 39-47
exploring 40, 41
**single hidden layer neural network
model** 138, 140
Stochastic Gradient Descent (SGD) 122

T

TensorFlow
about 1
future 147, 148
installation page 3
installing 2
installing, via CoCalc 6-10
installing, via pip 4, 5
main page 2
projects 149, 150
TensorFlow learn
about 117
logistic regression 120
reference link 117
setup 117, 118